Beyond Best

Peak Performance in Changing Times

Dr. Nell Rodgers

Awesome Press, Inc.
P. O. Box 1071
Decatur, GA 30031-1071

Rodgers, Dr. Nell M.
Beyond Best: Peak Performance in Changing Times

Layout: J. L. Saloff
Fonts: Garamond Premier Pro, President, Worstveld Sting
Cover Design: Copen Marketing & Design

10-Digit ISBN: 0-9745240-3-4
13-Digit ISBN: 978-0-9745240-3-0
Library of Congress Control Number: 2007902344

First Edition

Printed in the United State of America on acid free paper.

1.01

Dedication:

For all those who
honor my efforts,
give me their trust and
affirm my path.

Acknowledgments

A number of people stand out in their steadfast loyalty and support as I wrote Beyond Best.

My best friend and confidant, Charli Vogt, has, as always, given me unwavering moral support, unconditional love, and more than I ever hoped for in understanding and absolute honesty.

My formatter, Jamie Saloff, is astonishingly willing to do whatever is needed. Her optimism, consultation, understanding, and genuine attentiveness has gone beyond amazing. Her work reflects her love.

Vicki Sullivan gave me unending encouragement and sincere belief. Her optimism, consultation, understanding, inspiration, nudging and genuine attentiveness to both process and composition, provided the focus and motivation which enabled me to birth this work.

Sharon. K. Garner took on the formidable task of editing long pages of information and guiding me with gentle, positive suggestions.

The value of sisters and what they bring to each other has filled books. Mine, Thelma, Rachel and Ruth, have unceasingly given to me without asking why. They never stop believing in their sis.

What does one say about friends who are always with me, no matter what formidable task or crazy thing I attempt? These people, to me, are like brilliant stars in the darkest midnight sky: Dr. Theresa Pigott, Cindy Norlin, Donna Patrick, Ann McElfresh, Janet Londagin, Lisa Cotrell, Judy Dorman, Virginia Erhardt, Deborah Monroy, and Dr. Pat Gibson.

My writing group, Sylvia Sultenfuss, Fran Hagaman, Sharon Yarborough, Melinda Hunley, Robbie Gring Campbell, Najma Beresford and Jeanne Guthrie, has been a source of inspiration. They also remind me that writers are permitted moments of "insanity."

To all of you, I express and extend my deepest heartfelt appreciation.

Table of Contents

Introduction

For years, I saw in myself and my clients how, at times, we wanted to pursue one course of action, yet "discovered" ourselves on a different path. We laughingly said that it seemed as if the world was somehow plotting to thwart our success or shift our goals. As we sought fulfillment and chased our dreams, feedback sometimes indicated that we were engaged in incongruous or seemingly injudicious actions. That frustrating word, "self-sabotage" also made entrance from time to time. I now know that the world was not plotting against us. There is a reason for those annoyances and setbacks.

Personal laws determine our success or failure and dictate our choices. Each of us has an internal search engine at work 24 hours per day, 365 days per year. It is constantly scanning to match our internal programs to the external world. This automaton never takes a rest. As if that were not enough to run us amuck, most of us have, early on, been assigned roles that can camouflage our abilities and purpose. Thus, we grow up and step into our careers and family lives with a few strikes against us. Circumscribed truths can become our nemesis. Even though we feel excited, trusting and hopeful, even though we begin with resounding confidence, our personal empire can come crashing down. Occasionally, it is more of a clang than a crash. Still, our effectiveness gets tested and our resolve may be questioned. Some individuals actually lose their identity in their quest to find it. Many are pulled in the direction of the "truths" they were given instead of connecting with their own inner values and passion. They chase a phantom identity.

Alluring waves of promise, money, novelty or technology can be intoxicating. The challenge is to assume higher levels of responsibility commensurate with that freedom while standing in our *own truth* as we maintain our daily lives. Most of us have at least a few beliefs which can become adversaries. Even though we take responsibility and work hard, our beliefs and stories can become heavyweight challengers. In this book you will come to appreciate the value of fully understanding your intentions in relation to the beliefs you hold as truth. You will see how this understanding can be a surprising and impressive liberator. You will see that our rules are a part of who we are and recognize that this understanding alone can dramatically alter achievement and success. You will understand willing acceptance as well as willing resistance; how you are compelled to follow the rules when you, in fact, would much prefer doing something different

By and large, significant others thought they were giving us their first-class tools for living as we grew up. They decided for us, directed us, protected us and in the long run, gave us many of their beliefs, rules and ideas. The difficulty lies in the fact that the majority of us accepted them carte blanche. We took on assigned roles that remained intact into adulthood. You will learn how these assigned roles become reality; how an emotionally laden story becomes a guiding truth. You will understand when this is okay and how, at other times, that role or emotional truth keeps you from conscious desires, intention and dreams.

Many are *subconsciously* living out a parent's wish or following in someone's footsteps, while neglecting their own intuitive guidance and passion. Most people have become adept at socially accepted coping mechanisms. Although these ideas are acknowledged, there is little definitive written information which tells us how and why this happens. *Beyond Best* helps you understand that seeing a lesson within a situation does not necessarily mean that you learned from it. You will see that awareness in not enough to change how a person functions. Discussions among friends may bring clarity. Certainly there is value in clarity, but having clarity also does not equate resolution. One must go beyond understanding, awareness and clarity in order to effect personal shifts and transformation. *Beyond Best* demonstrates why this is true and shows you how to resolve personal issues. You will be shown how learning experiences set up behaviors which are related to external conditions and the ways in which those conditions monitor and automatically determine how we respond.

In addition to those external forces which imprint our lives, a Universal Choreography, as I like to call it, supports our actions and offers guidance via intuitive and other forces. It takes into consideration our linear thinking; our knowledge; our connection with Spirit, each other, and the Planet; our genetic heritage; our DNA; our beliefs; our perceptions; our Will; that elusive energy called life-force and all else, imagined, defined and undefined. As we search for the perfect transforming goal, that completely gratifying situation or seek an equalized emotional state, we tend to forget this. Here, you can learn how to tune in to your intuitive self.

Being human, to many, has come to mean "includes failure" and often provides an excuse when we do or say things we regret or which cause difficulty. Lack of success or defeat may or may not be related to the human predicament, per se. Because we are bound by our beliefs and perceptions, we, ourselves, can bind ourselves to outcomes.

Opening our lives to adventure and creative meanderings can get set aside in favor of a more comfortable, more common or less awkward path. Mostly, I think, this is because we have not known that there is no reason to let go of our uniqueness or our place in the world. We have not known that our stories hold us hostage and prevent the realization of our goals and dreams. This book gives insight and understanding of these concepts, and shows how, unwittingly, we stepped into the truth and course of others, often neglecting our own.

Beyond Best is about understanding how non-supportive truths and beliefs run our lives. It encourages you to create and bolster your own beliefs, emotionally disconnect from your stories, let go of assigned roles, and step into your own truth and identity. In my own journey, I discovered that my authenticity had been masked. In order to claim inner strength, gain clarity and thus step into my dreams, I had to determine my own truth. *Beyond Best* offers examples of how I and others have chosen to set our own destiny.

Fortunately for all of us, The Universal Choreography is designed to promote the creation of new dances. Our feet and our spirit can be set free. We can know our passion and throw ourselves fully into it. Nothing is more empowering than to let go of the stories which bind us to constricting beliefs and subsequent behaviors. Nothing is more freeing than seeing the world through different lenses or letting go of stereotypic and dogmatic perceptions. In doing so, we can let go of blame, fear, guilt, and shame. These hindrances can be replaced with curiosity, passion and creativity. We can be taken off of "automatic" and shifted into creative exploration of life and individual passion. I invite you to come along on this fascinating and enticing journey.

I

Part One

"Loyalty to petrified opinion never yet broke
a chain or freed a human soul."

—Mark Twain

1
Destiny Is an Illusion: Tell Everybody

PERCHED ON A MAMMOTH BOULDER IN THE VAST TEXAS desert, I huddled under my poncho, covering my backpack and myself as well as I could. The sudden squall of mixed rain, marble hail, frenzied lightning and thunder was fierce and somewhat frightening. There was no place to take refuge and I was extremely vulnerable. Pushing back my fear, I sang loudly, “Happy birthday to me, happy birthday to me,” forcing myself to believe I was okay, safe in the midst of danger. What I desperately wanted on this birthday was to keep my boots dry. Two toes were already sore. I knew the protocol for backpacking. Why had I not followed it?

The storm passed. I unfolded myself and assessed the damage: boots wet on one side, hat wrecked by hail, body and clothes wet from thighs downward, pack dry except for a few clothes on one side, food okay. Undaunted, I limped away from my roost. Only then did I remember that being on a boulder increased the potential of a lightning strike. What had I been thinking? Ordinarily, I wore an old fishing hat. What motivated me to wear a new straw hat of sentimental value that my poncho would not fit over? Why did I wear work boots instead of my hiking boots?

What prompted me to walk 75 miles alone in the wilderness during a time usually reserved for ritualistic celebration, and on the "big forty" as well?

What makes any of us knowingly cast aside our wisdom? Why do we forego logic or intuitive information and rush headlong into undesirable behavior? Why do we repeat unwanted patterns of behavior? To our amazement, we automatically do or say things that undermine that which we are striving to accomplish. We sometimes cripple our efforts at strategic moments. The begging question is, why? What makes us knowingly duplicate unwanted actions?* Comedians say, "Because we are dumb!" Scholars say, "We don't take the time and effort to think through the situation." Families will—well, let's not go there!

When we exhibit a behavior we thought we had conquered or annihilated, ruthless thoughts jam our heads as if the brain were searching for responses to a scholastic test in which all answers must be explained to Einstein. "What *were* you thinking?" "*Expletive*–I can't believe I did that *again!*" "What is *wrong* with me?" Most of us waste little time in pouncing on ourselves with labels such as "stupid thinking" or "dumb move." We find no answers to these seemingly rhetorical questions because they are not rhetorical. Answers do exist. However, they do not come in the expected form. We are usually consciously applying our intellect and rational thought to an illogical, irrational perspective. Mostly, though, we are asking the wrong questions. Those unwanted, often spontaneous behaviors almost always originate from a subconscious agenda. We automatically proceed, behave, function or react, and only after the fact, look for causal factors. It is probable that you have at some time, had thoughts or experiences such as:

---

* Throughout this book, discussions regarding behavioral patterns, reactions and automatic responses are seen as separate behaviors, unrelated to broad abusive addictions such as drugs, alcohol, sex, bulimia, anorexia, shopping, gambling and so forth.

"I knew I was driving fast, but I was in a hurry."
Result: a traffic violation ticket.

"I swore to myself I would always get everything in writing before I signed anything, but I broke my promise to myself."
Result: you are stuck with a deal you don't want.

"The community ***really needs*** *this project completed. I'm one of the few people who knows how to do it. I just couldn't say no."*
Result: you are on so many committees that you have no time for yourself or your family.

These kinds of responses stem from conflicting information. We "know" one thing but do or say another.

Thomas had risen through the ranks. Now the company was downsizing. He confided, "I'm being considered for promotion to director and a big fat pay raise." Thomas had no substantiating data for his claims. He connected his desire for promotion to a few overheard snippets of conversation. Imagine his surprise when he received notice he was being laterally transferred to the branch in Germany. Signs were evident, but Thomas's itch for a director's position and gloating to peers took over. Ya gotta watch that ego.

The above examples show how we operate from subconscious programs that cause us to continue on a path regardless of feedback. To cite a corporate example, Volkswagen of America had branded itself as building efficient, few-frills cars for "the people." They rushed to take on the next big thing and produced an SUV and a luxury sedan. They filled their basic models with plastic and padding that turned off a core constituency. They *reacted* to an industry phenomenon without fine-tuning to "the people." The Mini Cooper, simple, solid and small, filled the abandoned niche.

Volkswagen's actions could be logically, rationally and analytically validated. Each aspect of my seemingly misguided desert trek can be legitimately explained. I carefully planned my route, contemplated whether I would regret being alone when turning 40, deliberately wore a different hat because of my attachment to it, and chose the softness of work boots over hiking boots. Although I left the trailhead late, I could not know in advance that I would face a rattlesnake on the path and be forced to stand frozen in place for 20 minutes—every nerve on the alert, draining my energy and burning time. Thunderstorms are common in the desert, but the forecast predicted clear weather for the entire week Self-explanations such as these are usually boring and frustrating. We use them to tranquilize the chattering mind, absolve a bit of guilt or get us off the hook, since a few of the answers seem rational enough to account for unwanted behavior.

In my trek, I could make a case for coincidence and rotten luck. On the other hand, I *knew* the appropriate hat and shoes for trekking. I *knew* I would be alone on my birthday. I *knew* that anything can happen in a desert storm. I *knew* I needed to leave the trailhead by a certain hour. Why did I circumvent my own wisdom? In reality, the circumventing of my own wisdom had little, if anything, to do with some of my behavior.

Each of us has persistent subconscious patterns of behavior that ignore conscious, intellectual thinking. Yo-yo dieting,* yo-yo exercising, returning to unhealthy relationships, and repetitious battling with family or coworkers are broad representative examples. Most of us try again and again to interrupt certain behaviors. We very much want to remember to go to the gym, ignore the overly competitive colleague, stop kowtow-

* Clinical levels of addictions are excluded here. Although some of the same principles apply, more in depth discussion would be needed to explore those behaviors.

ing to the big boss, or let go of being hooked by a spouse's pugnacious behavior.

Sometimes we feel as if we are destined to be the victim, to put that proverbial foot into our mouth, or to do a particular thing. Over time we begin to believe that we are limited in our ability to control certain emotions or reactions. Because of the intense desire to erase or control those behaviors, we actually give credence to the notion that we have some sort of genetic blemish or inadequacy which compels us to perpetuate our conduct. Thoughts of DNA damage or a genetic heritage that compels you to eat boiled pickles in the presence of smoker's breath can seem to override rational thinking. "Maybe Dad was right. Maybe I did inherit my mother's, father's, uncle on his mother's side knack for screwing up. I am doomed."

If we could blame a debauched ancestor, or a lousy genealogical tree, we might feel better.

If we could blame a debauched ancestor or a lousy genealogical tree, we might feel better. Knowing that I inherited my Irish temper may help soothe my guilt after an angry outburst. I could believe that I am genetically designed in a way that saddles me with being a hostile old bag like my grandmother, or a sinister, unforgiving genius like my uncle. To live with such paradigms would mean we have no control over our destiny, that no change could occur in our behavior or our life.

The terrific news is that while our parents or a Significant Other (SO)[*] may be responsible for many of our conditioned reflexes, *destiny is an illusion*. Genes do not direct our lives. The interaction of our genes in relation to our environment determines who we are at any given moment. Noted cell biologist Bruce Lipton reiterates this when he states:

* Significant Other (SO) is used throughout this text to represent parents, other family members, extended family, or anyone who is in a position of authority, nurturing or guiding.

> "...a cell's life is controlled by the physical and energetic environment and not by its genes. Genes are simply molecular blueprints used in the construction of cells, tissues and organs. The environment serves as a 'contractor' who reads and engages those genetic blueprints and is ultimately responsible for the character of a cell's life. *It is a single cell's 'awareness' of the environment, not its genes*, that sets into motion the mechanisms of life." (Emphasis mine.) [1]

Persistent contention that we are victims of our genes, that our self-destructive or brilliant behavior is the result of our genetic heritage can, in itself, be a form of defeat. It is far more meaningful and valuable to understand that patterns of behavior and reactions are learned through our environment. Both our responses and our reactions stem from beliefs which are stored as programs within the subconscious mind. Teaching and modeling is the role our parents and SOs play in our so-called predestined behavioral codes of conduct, habits and performance. They show us how to respond and react. In fact, Significant Others often demand specific behaviors whether or not we want to behave as they ask, learn their way or accept their truth.

Here is more good news. Because they are learned, unwanted automatic reactions and behaviors can be erased and replaced with new paradigms of behavior regardless of your genetic heritage.

It is common knowledge that throughout life, especially in childhood years, our body-mind records what we do, what we perceive, how we respond, and all related emotions. If you have a pleasant, mouthwatering, anticipatory emotional association to chimichangas and koala fondue, you somewhere learned to have that specific response. Beyond your conscious desire, no matter what the circumstance, you will experience that engaging reaction until some emotionally charged incident changes it, or until the automatic reaction is purposefully erased from your subconscious. Since these reactions are reflexive in nature, this concept holds true regardless of whether it is held as a positive or a negative experience. Whether you testily, in a passionate moment, tell your boss, "No chance, Lance," or spontaneously take a chance on kissing your blind date, reflexive deeds occur aside from rational thinking.

Biochemical, structural and emotional elements of the body come together at the cellular level to form behavioral reactions. Each is related to specific experiences, especially those charged with emotion. I emphasize that either or both the emotions and the reaction may be experienced as positive or negative. An example would be getting a promotion but feeling angry about what had to be done to obtain it. The reverse is also true. A woman (or man) may judge a sexual overture as unacceptable, while at the same time feeling flattered they are still sexually appealing. All emotionally charged *reactions* stem from recorded belief programs within the physiological cellular structures of our bodies. These reactions can be triggered by any person, place, thing, situation or circumstance. The environment, not genes, initiates these programs.

Our internal computer is constantly scanning, programming and providing feedback. Think of it as a "brain-mind-gut-cellular-nervous-system-sensory-emotions-neuropeptide-DNA-systemic-biochemical-energetic-body information network." This neuro-physiological epicenter records every act, every thought, every feeling, every input. In short, we are continually either living our programs or being programmed. Our internal computer literally harbors everything. This includes what you consciously want, your grandmother's face, the time you wet your pants on the roller coaster, the Christmas you were forced to eat Aunt Etta's egg plant-carrot dumplings, the day you found a bird's nest, your first sexual experience, the tears of a broken heart, the joy of celebrating, *everything.*

Some experiences are recorded as memories only. They have no particular positive or negative charge. Other experiences stick. They become imprinted hardwiring in the body-mind. These imprints, not destiny, drive you to automatically behave in predetermined ways. You are programmed by and for specific events and particular people in your life. The facinating, as well as sometimes disturbing, phenomenon is that unless these programs are altered in some way, automatic behaviors and reactions repetitiously occur, wanted or unwanted. I have labeled this automatic, subconscious response epicenter the Cellular Response System (CRS). It is here that all programs/imprints are housed. Through the CRS, our programs compel us to maintain particular behaviors, values, principles, rules and various roles. They govern how we live, perform, conform, react and relate to others.

> You are programmed by and for specific events and particular people in your life.

When you have a "gut reaction" to something, when you maintain rules that make no logical sense, when you habitually repeat a behavior you would prefer to eliminate, you are usually experiencing an automated reaction through your Cellular Response System imprint.

For example, if your father was a podiatrist who became a "volcanic eruption" when seeing dirty feet or toenails, you may have learned never to go barefoot except on carpet, and to condemn dirt under toenails. If your father generated a program in your CRS, you may now become the "volcanic eruption" when your spouse or child has dirty toenails. In anger, you could threaten to bring out a hacksaw, a surgical scrub brush and Mr. Clean. These automatic reactions are under the control of the subconscious Cellular Response System. They are *not* controlled by conscious desire or intellect. All that matters is that toenails are clean. How others regard dirty toenails is immaterial. This is the reason we sometimes diligently try to stop a knee-jerk reaction, only to have it remain the same. This is why we insist beyond reason that things should be done in a particular way. The imprinted CRS gives its automatic reflexive reactions regardless of efforts to eliminate them.

Tom Peters, business management consultant, says that a big problem in business is that people in the thick of things tend to mistake their world for the whole world. In great part that's because of imprinted programs that drive us. Our beliefs are extremely personalized and specifically affect our perceptions.

Recently, I saw a man who refused to let his teenage daughter talk to him after 9 p. m. because he thought she was too emotional. With coaching, he let go of his unbending rule. He was surprised to discover that his daughter was not emotional, and in fact, he enjoyed their conversations. To his amazement, he began to learn more about her and felt a deeper connection which he immensely valued. Duh! This man's expectations and apprehension were based on an experience which got recorded as "truth" in his CRS. If he had called me, I could have told him that teenage girls can be emotional at any hour, in any place, and in relation to any conversation or situation.

This gentleman held his children as dear, but beliefs and perceptions in his CRS overrode that set of values. When we are acting with incompetence, rationalization, mediocrity, using questionable ethics or justifying behavior, it is generally because the CRS is engaged. It disregards integrity, logic, clarity and ethics because it is an automated system. A person can certainly also have beliefs which support these meritorious principles. The degree to which each is constant, however, is subject to the reactive programs of the Cellular Response System.

Certain events, especially emotionally charged ones, are recorded as unresolved issues in the CRS. At this point, destiny does make an entrance. You are destined to repeat these recorded patterns in an automatic, reflexive manner until the subconscious CRS hardwiring is altered. Learned rules, values, principles and roles—our perceptions—together with our conscious choices, control who we are and how we experience life.

Suppose you always feel nervous and automatically defend or justify your actions when a person of authority approaches you. The defense may be internal or audible. Either way, the internal dialogue is an attempt to convince yourself that you or your behavior is sanctioned. This automatic reaction, stemming from the CRS, will again and again repeat itself each time you are in the presence of authority figures. Fortunately, CRS reactions are not destiny in the truest sense of the word. You are not decreed by genetic heritage or a DNA strand to continue validating yourself with authority figures. Although the CRS is bound by its very mission to automatically keep the reaction alive as long as it retains that program, the program itself can be changed.

We sometimes think we are destined because our CRS dictates habitual, unwilled reactions. Marion is a mature, dynamic and successful psychotherapist, but she is held hostage by her inability to say no. Every day she teaches others to responsibly make decisions, including expressing a difficult no. She would like to practice what she preaches, but cannot. Her inability to say no rises from the strict rules of obedience laid down by her punitive father. Marion's CRS was programmed to say yes, to be obedient in order to avoid punishment. Of course, there is far more complexity to her programming, but, in short, she was programmed to obey. If her husband says, "We are going to the Mall of America for our vacation," she will go even though she dislikes shopping. If the proctologist says, "You must have this test," she must comply, although she would definitely prefer to give the test to the doctor.

Thinking it is destiny to pursue a specific course or do a certain thing is not truth. You may believe it is your destiny to help take care of servicemen. Therefore, you set up a proprietary chain of sales booths for hashish near U. S. Air Force bases in order to bring much needed R&R to the pilots. In this instance, you are probably also being stupid. My point in suggesting such an outlandish example is to spotlight that destiny is an illusion. We are slaves to our perceptions supported by our beliefs and CRS imprints. Dr Lipton's research has demonstrated that we literally seek environments which support the survival of our beliefs. If we are programmed for negative behaviors such as anger, fear and addictions, we will find them. If our CRS imprints call for positive behaviors such as hobbies, laughter and joy, we will migrate to that.

Whatever our course, it is the choices we make and clarity of action that creates our so-called destiny. When we veer off into automatic behaviors, the CRS is merely doing its thing, week after week, hour by hour. It reacts precisely according to its imprinted programs. Since this phenomenon occurs at the cellular level, you may feel as though you are somehow predestined. You can avoid that by changing your beliefs and perceptions. The exciting aspect of this phenomenon is that if your dad made you gargle before going on a date, you do not have to do that anymore. Of course, gargling before a big date may be a ritual that you would like to keep. That choice is yours. Do you realize how incredibly wonderful this is? This means that no one is genetically predetermined to be a jackass.

Fundamentals

Destiny is an illusion.

Arnold seemed destined to become a surgeon. His father and grandfather were physicians. His family expected that Arnold would follow their examples. Arnold wanted to be a classical pianist. However, his subconscious had been programmed in obedience and respect. His family, through expectations, set up a self-fulfilling prophecy phenomenon.

Medical school was tedious but Arnold completed his studies and is now a revered surgeon, but he is less than happy. This man's destiny was not to become a surgeon. Arnold's CRS overrode his desire to be a musician by directing his behavior and choices. His hope to pursue a career in music buckled in the presence of his CRS's automatic surrender to obedience and respect. His genetic brilliance would have lent itself to music or other chosen vocations as well as it has to the medical profession.

Of course, Arnold still has options. He could serenade his patients with a bit of Chopin before and after surgery. Obviously, he would either need a Steinway on wheels or a porter and gurney on standby at all times. The good news is, he would never have to audition.

Sorry, It's Not Your Genes: Environment and Perception Determine Destiny

ALTHOUGH GENES OFFER PERSONAL DESIGN, THEY DO NOT direct how we live or what we experience. The excuse "it's genetic" is as invalid as the notion that we must blindly follow our destiny. Our genetic heritage is merely a foundation and not a causative factor in our behavior. Yes, even the latest American Idol had to override and change CRS imprints related to auditioning, developing voice technique and being on stage. Specific genes are inherited. However, these genes are guided and customized by environmental experiences.

Numerous adopted children lead dramatically different lives purely because their environment and nurturing are different than if they stayed with their birth parents. A mother who is giving her baby for adoption says, "I want my baby to have the life I cannot offer it." She intuitively understands that her child will behave differently, that his/her life will be determined by new parents and new surroundings.

The rapidly growing field of Functional Diagnostic Medicine has learned it must integrate such data as the individual's environment, attitudes and beliefs into the diagnostic assay. Researchers in epigenetics are learning that there is more to genetics than sequenced DNA molecules. According to a report by the BBC, epigenetics:

> "... adds a whole new layer to genes beyond the DNA. It proposes a control system of switches that turn genes on or off—and suggests that things people experience, like nutrition and stress, can control these switches and cause heritable effects in humans.
>
> Professor Wolf Reik, at the Babraham Institute in Cambridge, has spent years studying this hidden ghost world. He has found that merely manipulating mice embryos is enough to set off switches that turn genes on or off.... His research has demonstrated that genes and the environment are not mutually exclusive but are inextricably intertwined, one affecting the other."[2]

Suppose your mother was a "neat freak" who required that you make your bed each morning. If she cultivated this habit in a manner that sparked emotions, which caused an imprint in your Cellular Response System, you will continue to make your bed each morning, but without joy. Your mother may die. Still you make your bed or suffer the consequences. What consequences? No bed police will be checking your home to see that all the beds are neatly made. Making the bed is an automated reaction that has been recorded in your CRS, a program that most likely includes guilt or fear. Until that emotionally charged pattern is settled, you are "destined" to make your bed each morning. Clearly, it is not genes inherited from your mother that perpetuates your compulsion to make your bed. Your behavior was learned, and you still operate from a child's position that you may get into trouble if you leave it unmade.

"Oh, sure," you say. "Of course! That's learned behavior. What about intelligence? Bright parents usually have bright children." Consider identical twin orphan children in a third world country. Neither is with their ancestral family. The genetic pool is basically the same. One child is adopted and taken away from the local culture. One remains in the birth country. The only difference is that one child is brought to another culture. This child, with the same genetic heritage and intellect is likely to be far more precocious and will develop talents far differently than the twin who was left behind. Studies with children in Harlem showed that those who received nurturing attention and genuine intellectual stimulus, excel. Others who were thought to be intellectually sharp, often achieved little.

The reaction of each child is based in the definition they have given the experience.

Why do these departures from so-called genetic heritage occur? Actually, they are not departures. Doctors Candace Pert and Bruce Lipton have validated that nurture determines and modifies the expression of genetic potential. It is a variation on the ol' "garbage in, garbage out" theory. One child is afraid of fireworks and lightning, whereas a sibling loves the excitement. The reaction of each child is based in the definition they have given the experience. Their perception of the event is based in the collective signals they have received from their environment and how they have learned to relate to those signals.

Duke University Professor H. F. Nijhout, reports in his research, "When a gene product is needed, a signal from its environment, not an emergent property of the gene itself, activates expression of that gene."[3]

Imagine the difference in the responses of a Watts teenager and a teenager from Hollywood to the question, "How would you like it if I told you-know-who about you-know-what?" Each has their personal way of responding. This is universal. To a tailor, a zipper problem means one thing. Those same words take on an entirely different meaning for President Clinton.

Human beings are objects. (I mean no offense to celebrities.) Objects reflect, absorb or generate. As we grow from birth to adult we are constantly absorbing and reflecting. One child may reflect family rules by engaging in stubbornness and refusal to adhere to the given code of conduct. Another may become so rule-conscious that s/he is too anxious to step into the possible human s/he could become.

Body cell receptors "read" the environment and translate signals into behavior. Each individual will conscript reactions in their CRS that are specifically related to family members and Significant Others. Stories abound of supposedly retarded or borderline intelligence children who, after being placed in a new environment, generate amazing lives. Nurturing in the presence of supportive guidance directed their information processing and "custom developed" the genes of these children. Had they been neglected and abused, their behavior would reflect this through a continuing presentation of "retarded" behavior. Behavior and demeanor is reflective of environmental stimulus.

Behavior and demeanor is reflective of environmental stimulus.

Most of us understand that we copy the behaviors of Significant Others. A father who is an outstanding mechanic will teach his son some tricks of the trade. If the son is interested in mechanics, takes on the business and follows in his father's footsteps, we say, "He has the genes for 'mechanic-ing,' just like his father." The son may, indeed, have genes that promote dexterity and provide intellect for "mechanic-ing." However, he also has the genes that would allow him to become a polar bear eyebrow specialist had he been placed in that environment.

Research has repeatedly demonstrated that individual reactions at the cellular level, particularly to family and SOs, not genes, create the benchmark for personal behavior. In other words, our programming and conditioning determines our conduct, habits and performance.

Peak Potentials guru T. Harv Eker, in *Secrets of the Millionaire Mind* says, "Give me five minutes and I can predict your financial future for the rest of your life."[4] He can do this by identifying the individual's "money and success blueprint" which is ingrained in the person's subconscious mind. Eker reiterates that you can know everything about sales, negotiating, business, and the world of finance, but if your CRS is not hardwired for a high level of success, forget it, unless, of course, you identify and change that blueprint.

Expectations housed in our beliefs play a major role in the development of our behaviors. Both the expectations of ourselves and those of SOs come into play. When we have expectations, we anticipate reward, punishment, praise or criticism related to a particular behavior.

Betty Sue expects praise and public recognition when she donates money for a new church organ. If the minister fails to fulfill her expectation, she may be disappointed, angered or sullen. Depending upon the degree of her emotional response to the unfulfilled expectation, she may never again make a donation, or in a moment of passion, leave the church. Such reactions generally are more emotionally painful to the person who holds the expectation than to those around them.

Expectations placed by Significant Others, particularly in children, are a frequent source of internalized behavior. Through authoritative positioning, a child is obligated to a specific response or required to follow explicit rules of conduct. The SO almost always believes they know what is best or right. They attempt to control even if only because the action is believed to be advantageous for the other person. All too often, expectations of the SO reflect the belief that "my way" is the correct way, the best way, the only way or "just how it is." These people want others to be independent—as long as you do everything they say to do. Respect can mean "never disobey me." Expectations can become rules.

I remember that as a graduate student I was often told, "You are invited and expected to attend." Imagine my surprise! I previously had the silly notion that an invitation meant my presence was optional. The things one learns in school can be amazing.

When a Significant Other is determined to control a situation or the outcome of a conflict, the circumstances are often charged with emotions. In my example of "being invited and expected to attend," I became angry at being forced to go to a costly retreat in which I had no interest. No choice was given. I would go or pay whatever punitive price the professor chose to mete out. Here are examples of times when highly emotional reactions may be present:

- The Significant Other has definite, unwavering ideas about right and wrong in the presence of conflicting ideas from another. Jerry wants to read the Harry Potter books. His father's religious beliefs say, "Over my dead body!"

- There is a difference of opinion as to who has authority in deciding upon a particular behavior, such as what to eat. Doesn't every kid hate green peas and liver?

- A person has a keen desire to do something different than what they are told they must do. She's in "luv" at age 13, but her parents declare she will not date until age 16.

- An individual does not want to do what the SO requests. He is the starting pitcher for his team but Mother says he must do homework before ball practice. A daughter is required to skip a piano lesson in order to baby-sit.

- The SO insists that an individual do something they dislike. "You *will* stay in school and you *will* make good grades," or "You *will* hug me good-bye when I drop you off at school."

These individuals can learn how to behave in order to avoid punishment and criticism. They also learn which behaviors bring reward and praise, as well as how to circumvent demands or requests. When an unresolved emotional hook-in is added to this complicated equation, cell receptors record it. Later, when that individual is in a similar situation, they will automatically revert to the learned (expected) reaction.

"I hate school!" says the baseball player. Mother's response is, "You'll hate not playing ball more." The kid uses his allowance to hire someone to write his homework papers while he goes to baseball practice. He has learned to surreptitiously outwit authority. Unless the conflict is resolved, this behavior will continue into adulthood, even in environments where the behavior makes no logical sense. When the things he wants in life seem unobtainable, he will go undercover to get them. Many of us still refuse to eat green peas, liver and onions.

The Cellular Response System does not turn off. It is a hardwired slave to constant assessing, recording, storing and reacting. Genes can be turned on and off throughout a lifetime. Grandma Moses began painting in her 70's. *AARP The Magazine* is replete with stories of older people who have dramatically altered their lives by learning new skills or pursuing unconventional activities. Most people never question their programs. They follow the same old patterns and stick with the same outmoded beliefs and values which may or may not serve their best interest. I have a friend who is quite proud of the fact that he has never had a recording of any kind, never owned a telephone answering machine, cell phone or a computer. He also believes he must accept whatever life hands him. I, on the other hand, never want to be stuck in a rut or in dull routines. In my 60's I enrolled in a stand-up comedian's class. At "graduation" each of us performed at a comedy club. My standing ovation is an exhilarating memory that I cherish. At age 70, I struck up a friendship with a 79-year-old woman during a ropes course. Our excitement was immeasurable. We both refuse to permit boring CRS reactions to rule us. None of our siblings with the same genetic base are doing these things. Is it not exciting that everyone has the capacity to shift their thinking or rewrite personal scripts?

No matter what genes you possess, changed thinking and new behavioral habits send new and more diverse signals to both your subconscious and your conscious brain. This is not an issue of hunting for old childhood stuff, and psychotherapy is absolutely not required. It *is* a matter of consciously sending new information to the CRS. It *is* utilizing original thinking, focusing on redesigning behaviors, and defusing emotional charges. It *is* letting go of outmoded learned responses. It *is* taking responsibility to consciously choose how you perceive and relate to your environment. It *is* knowing that genetics do not determine your life.

Quantum physics discloses that the observational mind is an explicit and major component of our reality. It also verifies that perception determines which genetic buttons get activated. Any individual can walk away from alleged "genetic makeup" or professed "destiny."

Although we cannot dismiss her talent, Madonna could have chosen to be a sensational Clean Air Turbulence Consultant. Her perception of her environment along with subsequent choices determined her fate. Madonna's father required his children to take music lessons. She convinced him to let her take ballet lessons instead, then moved to New York to pursue a career in dance. While dancing on tour, she became involved with musician Dan Gilroy. Later, they formed a rock band. From there, well, you know Madonna's fame. Had she been orphaned or lived on a farm, even with the same genes, it is unlikely that she would have become the highest earning female vocalist of all time. Her responses, her choices and her career would have been entirely different.

Let's put this into perspective. So your father was a sex therapist, your mother raised Angora rabbits, and your grandfather was an esteemed spiritual leader. You may have your mother's light hair and dreamy blue eyes, and the quick Irish temper of your father. Still, what matters in terms of your destiny is the kind and degree of nurture you have experienced, along with the unresolved issues that still hang out in your Cellular Response System. CRS change is what delivers us from temper tantrums, unwanted behavior, family drama and the drive to fulfill a destiny which may have been defined by a SO. Shifts in the CRS are created through specific reprogramming, elimination of old thinking, letting go of emotional hook-ins to past wrongs or disappointments, and consistently embracing new, noncharged thought patterns. You may never again eat rabbit, become secretive with your sex life, ignore spiritual development. Conversely, you may become a promiscuous chef who publishes a book of gourmet recipes for cooking rabbit. Whatever you do, your perception of your environment will determine your reality and your destiny. When perceptions change, life changes occur. Your genes are not in charge. Your infamous ancestors may supply a genetic framework. Your Tribe may pass on specific genes. However, you are responsible for their activation.

Fundamentals

Environmental experiences and influences, through cell receptors, determine which genes are activated.

Early marriage and a tight budget kept Margaret from higher education. Clerical jobs were boring. A benefactor helped Margaret fulfill her dream of a college education at age 49. At her first school assignment, every teacher had to take a rotation with less-gifted children. Margaret was given those children who were known to be "slow" in mathematics. Her excitement, her determination to do an outstanding job, and her willingness came together to nurture and guide these labeled youngsters.

With pictures, stories, interactive teaching, listening, praise, nurturing, and Margaret's personal investment, her "precious children" began to learn mathematics. They won recognition as a class for outstanding performance, outperforming other classes. The "dumb kids" became the "bright kids"! This was neither a case of a self-fulling prophecy nor an overnight sensation. It was a case of different environmental perceptions coupled with nurturing.

Being the grandchild of Albert Einstein will not mean you are a brilliant mathematician. On the contrary, you may choose to be a beach bum to avoid publicity and family pressure. It's your choice and your decision. Albert would probably be happy to encourage you in choosing for yourself.

Automation Never Exhibits Wisdom: It Don't Have None

THE SUBCONSCIOUS CANNOT BE SEEN, DISSECTED, touched or contained. Yet it is responsible for all those functions which are not controlled by the conscious mind. Yep, all of them, including such things as warts, ringing in the ears, impatience at the checkout line, intolerance and kleptomania. By design, like a computer—an overused metaphor, but true nonetheless—the subconscious performs either through programming or a conscious directive. This permits bodily functions to perform in harmony and as they are intended to operate, both individually and as components of systems. These functions are natural. The subconscious also "learns" how to execute particular commands. This hardwiring tells the Cellular Response System when to turn on the butterflies in the stomach, how to "defend" against being judged or ridiculed, when to have an anxiety attack, when to display self-righteousness, when to be stingy, when to be autocratic or romantic. In short, the data we accept into our cells automatically provides reactions that kick in under singular, circumstantial and definitive moments. *The CRS responds systematically and mechanically whenever the same or similar conditions occur which were present at the time the hardwiring was installed.* This is especially true when related or limiting emotional situations are replicated. It *must* respond in the same manner again and again because the emotional experience(s) have been caught in the psychosomatic network. Another way of saying this is, "What you see is what you get and, just like my daddy, I won't hesitate to embarrass myself exactly like he used to." The subconscious is incapable of discernment. Otherwise, the liver might be arguing with the pancreas when insulin levels vary, or the lungs might refuse to give oxygen in the presence of sexual excitement.

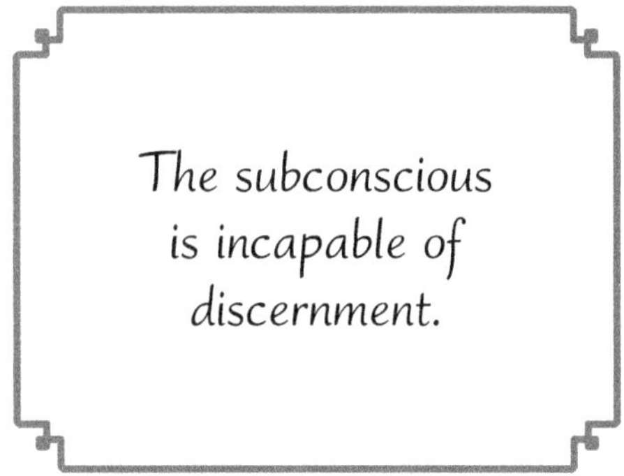

We do possess free will. We can use our conscious mind to choose what we desire. We have the option of how and whether we wish to respond to most circumstances. We have the cleverness and capacity to respond creatively and spontaneously to our environment. Our conscious abilities are keen. However, in order for choice and spontaneity to occur in the presence of the Cellular Response System's automated reactions, we must be alert and fully conscious. I am not speaking of being awake and functioning. By fully conscious I mean that in addition to being aware we must also be able to, within the moment, observe, evaluate and decide. Some aspects of this process take practice, but it can happen in a millisecond once we are cognizant and focused.

Malcolm Gladwell in *Blink: The Power of Thinking Without Thinking* describes how the first two seconds of looking can be a decisive glance that knows. He draws on cutting-edge neuroscience and psychology to show that the subconscious enables us to determine things in the blink of an eye. If we are less than fully conscious, a mechanical playback from the CRS can drive our responses irrespective of conscious preferences.

This is especially true in emotional reactions. Full attention is required. Otherwise, hardwired emotions pull us forward by anticipating a future outcome or thrust us backwards to old, unwanted reactions. The frustrating thing is that these automated reactions are not a part of our conscious thinking. We can be programmed to the extent that we actually believe we are making a conscious choice when we are not.

Celestine consistently gets angry because she believes her mother never hears her. For 50 years she has struggled with this. Celestine's CRS has so many automated reactions at the ready, it is difficult for her to realistically observe her behavior in relation to her mother. When they are together her mother constantly pushes Celestine's emotional buttons and Celestine, one more time, responds in the same old way. Anyone who replicates her mother's button-pushing behaviors elicits the same reaction. At 80, her mother is unlikely to change. In order for Celestine to respond instead of react to her mother, she must eliminate the emotional data that was hardwired early in life. She also must accept that the responsibility for creating a different reaction is hers, not her mother's. As one of my patients once said, "Ain't nobody gonna change nobody else."

Celestine is smart, wise and discerning. But when her CRS picks up the message through circumstantial data that she is encountering someone who refuses to listen or discounts her knowledge, there is no weighing of circumstances. Before an eye can blink, Celestine's CRS mobilizes the "appropriate" emotional reaction. It does not possess the judicious ability or discernment that Celestine, in her conscious mind, possesses. *The CRS has no wisdom*. This is the reason we end up asking ourselves why we did such a stupid thing, why we responded in an unnecessarily hostile manner, or why we behaved in a way we ordinarily would not behave.

All of us have similar programs ingrained within our CRS. Many individuals know their behavioral reactions even if they do not understand why they occur. At intervals, we would like to wish them away or choose antithetical alternatives. What is not prevalent in the thinking of most people is the fact that the Cellular Response System experiences these established operations as truths. We do not understand that we are responsible for changing any program that kicks into gear in the presence of specific circumstances.

It is important to remember that the subconscious is mechanical in its function. It does not think, assimilate, ponder, evaluate, choose or make decisions. Resembling an automaton, the CRS responds specifically according to encoded, imprinted instructions. In other words, you may have kissed your family good-bye as you moved into adulthood, but mom and dad are still with you. They have plopped their rules and preferences into your Cellular Response System, which holds them in residence inside your cells. Like a vulture on a dead carcass, those rules and beliefs will not voluntarily leave nor will they stop hounding you. You must evict the SOs who figuratively live inside before you can get different reactions from your subconscious.

Unlike the conscious mind, the subconscious cannot assess a situation or determine an appropriate response. Absence of wisdom in the CRS eliminates discrimination, cognizance and ingenuity. It has no insight or reasoning ability. Although we live in an age that espouses antidiscrimination, we do not need indiscriminate reactions. In fact, those who are totally indiscriminate end up in a rubber room at the funny farm. Letting the subconscious run our lives is tantamount to a planned reconnaissance meeting with a death adder. Like the coiled snake, the CRS is excellent in its power of execution. It provides automated reactions in a nanosecond that can then be executed before the conscious mind is aware that a reaction is present.

The CRS is self-regulating, spontaneous and consciously involuntary. If self-effacement is hardwired, you will find situations and ways to create it. Everything from pomposity, humility, aggressiveness, laziness, confidence, threats, optimism, charity, depression, anger and evasiveness to hyperactive behavior is recorded in the Cellular Response System. Occasionally, reactions can be related to chemical imbalances, but the ordinary reactions and behaviors that seize our attention usually are the result of an unresolved conflict or prior repetitive indoctrination.

Think of a time when you became aware that your face was already flushed before you realized you were angry. Initially, there was no awareness of the rising heat. It is possible you were unaware of why you became angry until after the fact. Or, consider a time when you blurted out words and later wished you had torn your tongue out of your face. In a split instant, you knew that no logical or wise person would ever make such a statement, especially in the presence of your idol, your pretentious boss or your staunch enemy. Ah, the CRS is in full force with its protective functional perceptions. You must react with foot-in-mouth confidence because your very cells have been instructed to do so. I have named these automated CRS behaviors *Auto-Reactions* because in these situations your subconscious is on "automatic-reaction overdrive." Since the subconscious has no wisdom, there is no way for you to win when these Auto-Reactions (AR) bolt forth. Replacement, override or elimination of the beastly little program that sucks you into the "What was I thinking" abyss is your only salvation.

Fundamentals

The subconscious has no wisdom.

Kenny had a speeding ticket. As he stood before the judge, he muttered, "I think you should gimme a break." Mama stared straight ahead. A few spectators snickered.

Judge: "Excuse me?"

Kenny: "Uh, I don't think I should git a fine. It was late night and nobody else wuz on the road."

Judge: "Would you please repeat what you just said?"

Kenny: "Yeah. I don't think I should git a fine. It was late night and nobody else wuz on the road. At least, reduce the fine. The patrolman was hidin' just trying to catch people." (Duh!)

Judge: "Turn around and look at the back of the room."

Kenny turned around, giving a huge sigh.

Judge: "Look at all those people. Every one of them probably thinks they are a special case. But I'll tell you something. When you break the law, that does *not* make you special."

Kenny; (facing the judge): "But there wudn't nobody else around, and it was really late at night." He continued to argue as the judge became more agitated.

Kenny was fined the maximum and had extra points against his license. This man consistently doomed himself. Two people prior to him had been given reprieve.

Kenny takes the role of victim, thinking he deserves special attention. His CRS did not have wisdom or discernment to behave differently with a judge who held all the cards. Wanna bet that mama had something to do with his, "treat me special" program?

4 Persistent Reactive Behaviors Can Spoil Your Fun: Stop! If You Want to

A FEW YEARS AGO, A SERVICE MAN SAW THE TANKLESS water heater in my home. He asked how I liked it. "It's great," I said. "We love it!" Even as I spoke, I knew some part of me was giving an automatic response. Overall, we are pleased. However, the whole truth is that there are several things we dislike about it. Was my answer a lie? Was I sacrificing my integrity? Was I saving face? You might ask, "Who gives a blue rat's tail about such a small indiscretion?"

It did not genuinely matter what I told the man. Of greater significance was its relevance to my personal goal of impeccable integrity. Hiding the whole truth was a subtle Auto-Reaction. My CRS held a multifaceted gotta-do-it-right, look-good, show-that-you-are-smart, be-perfect program. The CRS is constantly scanning and recording data which it regards as truth. It does not forget. In this circumstance, mine apparently read, "Must look good." My conscious intention for impeccable integrity was in conflict with my CRS program. The reactive statement was associated with a past event which deemed that I must do the right/smart thing. In 2006, Merriam-Webster's online Word of the Year was "truthiness." It is defined as 1: "truth that comes from the gut, not books." 2:

"the quality of preferring concepts or facts one wishes to be true, rather than concepts or facts known to be true".[5] I *wished* my statement to be the truth in that moment.

At seemingly the most inopportune time, we will reflexively do something which we later think is stupid, inappropriate or wrong. This can happen when we are joyful or composed. It can happen during times of adversity, challenge or neutrality. There is no statute of limitations on when, how, frequency of, or expanse of the repetitious patterns we exhibit. We may hold as reality that we have stopped a particular behavior, such as bickering. We may think we will never again exhibit a behavior which has embarrassed or caused us emotional pain. We may consciously believe that we are "above" certain behaviors, such as telling lies. Actual experiences tell a different tale. Since the CRS incontrovertibly responds, we find ourselves doing the same old thing one more time. Afterward, we tend to sit in judgment of our actions because other CRS imprints lead us to think that we have been bad or have done the wrong thing.

Judgment of the self is an interesting concept. We can judge ourselves to be iniquitous in some contexts or competent and wonderful in others. What I speak of here is different than knowing which things you excel at; when it is best to hand the job or responsibility to another person; when you are less than efficient; or, when you just plain stink at doing a particular task. I am referring to those relentless self-judgments that are laced with emotion. You know, those that drive our self-concept and cause us to label ourselves as inferior or grandiose; blundering or cocky and self-centered; "dumb" or superior. I mean those CRS-wired self-judgments that seem never to take a sabbatical.

Throughout life, notably in the early years, we base our judgment and value of what we can do and who we are upon our perception of what we believe others think of us. The judgment can get confused with our moralistic thinking as well. How incompetent is that? And how did we come to this?

Your parents may have modeled angry outbursts. As an adult, you subscribe to an etiquette that denounces such behavior. Yet you, too, have angry outbursts and seem unable to control when or where they occur. The related internal dialogue and feelings can be confusing, especially when you make the effort to stop and the outbursts continue. Failed attempts to change cause us to self-judge and to be unforgiving of ourselves. We can come to believe that we are unchangeable or have a bad streak. During this time, it is beneficial to look at personal beliefs to determine the role of your CRS in this self-judgment Auto-Reaction.

Failed attempts to change cause us to self-judge and to be unforgiving of ourselves.

Ruby walked up to the security guard on the subway platform and asked to borrow his bullhorn. Surprisingly, he handed it over. Ruby held the horn up and said, "Attention everyone. Listen up! I am here to declare that I love my husband more than anyone else in the world, and I will love him until the day I die. I want everyone to know that!" Her husband turned a glowing red. Karl was embarrassed by her public proclamation.

In observing the CRS of each, one might say that Ruby was perfectly okay. She laughed and felt exhilarated. There was no negative belief in her CRS related to "telling the world" she loved her husband. It was fun.

Karl, on the other hand, experienced a spontaneous, reflexive action to his wife's behavior. Somewhere in the past, Karl has been embarrassed, perhaps ridiculed, in a similar manner. When current circumstances replicated the old event, the unresolved emotional imprint caused an automatic embarrassment. Even though Karl may have felt proud that his wife loves him so much, his CRS overrode that feeling with an Auto-Reaction. Some will say that Karl will always be easily embarrassed, that it's just his nature. The truth is, if he prefers a different response in analogous circumstances, and he may, given who his wife is, Karl can immediately have it by resolving the initial issues which imprinted his cell memory. This would relieve his CRS of the obligatory response.

Giving lots of technical data here would probably bore you worse than watching a shoe polishing demonstration in the Antarctic. Still, some understanding of how CRS imprinting occurs is beneficial. For simplicity, let's say that the cells and neurons of the body can take on charges. The programmable "hard drive"—the CRS—can actually download emotional information and beliefs to receptor cells and neuronal tracts. These downloads, because of their charges, become fundamentally hardwired within the receptors. They then become stimulus-response behaviors.

In everyday life, these charges are frequently referred to as someone having "pushed your buttons." I know a board director who often gets "set off" when discussing opposing issues, has an angry outburst, then "kicks 'em out" of his office. He asked a peer to give a code word in those moments as a reminder that he is to remain calm. He is aware. He asked for help. Still, he says, "I just can't stop myself." This man's internal hardwiring is sabotaging his achievement. Uncovering or becoming aware of subconscious stimulus-response behaviors does not mean you need psychiatric sessions or that you must lie on an analyst's couch until it is rump-sprung. It does mean that you have a choice. The charges can be removed, and in so doing, the cellular signals

The charges can be removed, and in so doing, the cellular signals can be changed.

can be changed. However, if you think the couch would bring reprieve, by all means give it a try.

Understanding that we have amazingly large numbers of imprints in the CRS is germane to championing superior performance. When we Auto-React rather than consciously choose or decide, we are performing mechanically and habitually instead of creatively or purposefully. Occasionally, this is fine. Often, though, Auto-Reactions take on increased significance because of the weight they carry. An imprint underlying the attempt to be all things to all people, for example, can produce havoc and actually cause physical harm because of accompanying stress and perpetual action. This individual could have been the "keeper of the family," perhaps backed up by abuse. Another person may have a similar program because of attempts throughout childhood to get much-wanted love from a parent. Both are equally bound and still operate under personal laws laid down in early life. A single overwhelming emotionally charged experience can set up an AR of mammoth proportions or one that seems insignificant. By the same token, a significantly troublesome pattern can stem from a seemingly small issue. The impact rests within each individual's perceptions.

Trent climbed the ladder of success quickly, but now, he was having increasing difficulty. He thought this was connected to his recent divorce. Trent loves family and cherishes his father. Yet, after his divorce, he would not connect with his parents. He refused to answer their phone calls and completely stopped his frequent visits to their home. Trent's internal struggle was intense. Finances were arduous because of child support and court costs, but he would not accept money from his family. He no longer attended church and almost lost his home. He desperately needed a new vehicle. Still, he would not talk to or accept help from his parents. Trent's Cellular Response System had been majorly activated. When the unresolved pattern was isolated, it seemed almost trivial in comparison to current conditions. As a child, he had failed his father, whom he idolized, and thus experienced his father's quiet, but notable disappointment. Trent's young mind decided he was not a good son.

Presently, Trent knew instinctively how disappointed his father would be, because of religious beliefs, to learn of his divorce. He also knew that his father had resolutely withstood many intense ordeals to preserve his own marriage. Based on his emotionally laden childhood experience, Trent again saw himself as a "no good" son. This caused him to ignore the depth of his father's love. He could not focus on his parents' demonstrated willingness to do anything possible for their children. Trent's CRS automatically responded to the replication of events associated with having disappointed his father early in life. He could not face him now. The imprinted, unresolved childhood event preempted everything. Trent's Auto-Reaction actually kept him from receiving love and support at a critical time. This example clearly shows how ARs can interrupt our lives and affect our performance.

Many unresolved experiences are far more intense, such as severe accidents, child abuse, sexual assault, adoption, being jilted, having a parent never express their love. Any one or all can be hardwired to establish deleterious Auto-Reactions. Mother Teresa would want a word of hope here. It bears repeating that not all CRS programs stem from or create negative experiences. A favored student has a teacher who frequently brags on them, rewards them for outstanding performances and insists that they always do their best. Beliefs about competence and skill are being imprinted. The program could be desirable, or overbearing and inappropriate. Either way, this individual would be compelled to do their best in the presence of Significant Others. This may or may not be supportive. Doing your very best as a fortuneteller could be potentially catastrophic depending upon what you saw in your crystal ball.

There are as many unresolved issues as there are combinations of relationships and experiences. Some people relish the exploration of childhood memories. Others have the feeling that life is too short to spend time delving into the past. Your standing on this issue is directly related to your own beliefs. That's okay. I repeat, you do not have to tearfully spill your life history, lie on a couch hysterically reliving your life traumas or go on a spiritual pilgrimage to Machu Picchu. You are not "dysfunctional" or "predestined."

Although the Cellular Response System is unbending in its hard-wired reactions, it is your slave. When you program it to jump, it will not pause to ask, "How high?" It merely begins jumping when triggered. You have told it what to do and how to act based upon your perceptions. It responds accordingly. That's a huge reason repeated patterns of behavior experienced over a period of time come to be viewed as permanent or inevitable. Still, you have the option of programming "respond creatively" instead of "jump."

Attempting to *consciously* control your Auto-Reactions would be akin to trying to stop a politician from shaking hands or talking during a preelection tour. Observe the *circumstances* in which you see unwanted behavior in yourself. Stop trying to consciously control the reaction. You are the driver of the car, however, the controls are not in the trunk. Check out your programming.

Fundamentals

Spontaneous, reflexive actions occur in response to particular sets of present-time circumstances associated with prior emotionally charged, unresolved experiences.

Mona has a private practice. Her clients appear to love her and consistently tell her how valuable her work is. She perceives miracles walking out the door. This healer holds several degrees, has 30 years of experience, is a powerful communicator and is, by her own admission, loved by almost all who know her.

There is every reason to believe that Mona is successful. Appointments surge and wane, as they do in private practices. However, whenever Mona's practice numbers wane, she immediately begins thinking she has nothing to offer, *believing* that is the reason for fewer appointments. No amount of conversation can convince her otherwise. Her perception is clearly misaligned with reality.

Mona's mother consistently withheld love and stood in competition with Mona's every accomplishment. Mona was expected to do better and more than her siblings. Her parents disallowed her dream vocation and, instead, sent her to medical school. Mona's CRS says, "I am not good enough. I can never have what I want. I'm an imposter."

Until Mona's CRS is changed, she could skydive from the U. S. Space Station, bringing moon rocks in her pockets, live to tell about it, and still, she will automatically respond that she is not good enough or has nothing to offer.

5 Driving Beliefs Do Just That: Who Is Your Chauffeur and Who Hired 'Em?

Reality is created by validation. Repetitious reactions and messages set beliefs which become our truth. Allison Armstrong, in *Keys to the Kingdom*, speaks of how, during World War II, large numbers of women went to work. They became responsible for basic things concerning survival and thus took on an inherent importance. Women discovered they were smart and capable heroes. Many did not want to go back to a life that seemed less important.

The men returned with expectations of a normal life, but women were unwilling to give up their newly acquired importance. Men were unconvinced and the "righteous battle" began. Men became the enemy who must be *in*validated, because women wanted to be validated. Today, the aggregate subconscious of women holds as truth that men are the enemy because their collective subconscious recorded a Driving Belief that sustains women's hypercritical assumptions about men. Through the years, a reality has been created by repetitious validation. Attempts to "undo" this reality—that men are "pigs"—have, for the most part, been futile.

The Cellular Response System is meticulous in maintaining the reality it has been given. It literally validates what we perceive as reality, regardless of the truth. If the CRS has been given no instructions regarding a person, place, thing or event, it will ignore the situation and allow us to creatively and consciously follow our passion or obtain our goal, even if it is ridiculous or self-defeating. It will also assist us in making a fool of ourselves. This could explain those golden moments of unexpected and embarrassing microoutbursts during the training sessions led by your rival.

Years ago, when teaching at a university, I often got a rise from students when stating that the reason we communicate is to get someone to do something. Most saw that reasoning as selfish and untrue. Southern women would *never* forthrightly manipulate another into *doing* something every time they conversed with them. I'll be lenient and say, "And I've never eaten a slice of boloney." Their reality disallowed my concept of communication.

When bodywide neuropeptide systems get "hardwired," that information has been accepted as truth and reigns supreme in the subconscious. To the CRS this archival soapbox data is a reality that must be maintained. That's the reason your exasperating mother-in-law (or father-in-law—let's be nongender-biased) can efficiently and effectively strip you. Consciously and subconsciously, s/he has, with greater than satellite-antenna accuracy, observed and carefully collected data from you. Consciously and subconsciously, s/he is recording your modus operandi, your reality. Incredibly, her/his CRS aligns with your CRS and its perceptions. Once your automatic behavioral responses have kicked in a few times in her/his presence, you are a walking infomercial that screams, "Push this button. I will respond precisely on cue, now! Watch me crumble." Then, with laser sharpness, you are brought down. Her/his cool, autocratic armchair presence discerns the precise moment and action that will call forth from deep inside you that which you most do not want.

The subconscious never attempts a communication. It merely mechanically provides knee-jerk Auto-Reactions that pop forth like skyrockets. I chose the label Auto-Reactions *because* you have no premeditated conscious control over them. They occur when you least expect them, or passionately wish that they would not. When they suddenly appear, you are rarely in control. If fingers grew back, you might just chew off one in those moments.

Like it or not,
these Driving Beliefs
are intensely manifest
throughout our generic
identity.

Why is this important? Why does it matter if you and your mother-in-law routinely disagree or ignore each other? How does this relate to achievement and performance? How can Auto-Reactions keep you from your goals? One reason to disengage with your mother-in-law is to satisfy your own curiosity as to who she would deplore, judge or reprimand if you failed to take the bait. However, a more beneficial advantage of understanding ARs is because of the fundamental postulates which direct them. Encompassing, personalized events can turn into beliefs that propel our perceptual reality. Emotional Reality, in turn, provides central encoded instructions that can drive our lives. I call these personality pervasive convictions Driving Beliefs. Like it or not, these Driving Beliefs are intensely manifest throughout our generic identity. So who is your chauffeur and who hired 'em?

In emotional passion, Simon's mother called him stupid even though he was intellectually keen. If something went wrong and Simon was involved or nearby, she told him how stupid he was. She lashed out with comments such as, "I don't know how I could have such a stupid child." I think you see the stupid person in this scenario. Simon's inability to successfully ward off his mother's powerful accusations eventually embedded a Driving Belief that he is in some way stupid. As he matured and entered the workplace, he easily found jobs and delivered excellent work. But, consistently, at some point in each place of employment, he exhibited "stupid" behaviors that affected his performance rating, caused disciplinary action or resulting in his being fired.

Driving Beliefs are central, core, compelling personal laws. They cause us to behave, say and do specific things methodically and on cue, and are so pervasive that we rarely have awareness of their existence. Since they operate through Auto-Reactions, they cause us to maintain plateaus of specific behavior. We do not zealously go past a Driving Belief. They are the emotional skeleton of the CRS and provide a somewhat hidden agenda that compels everyday life. Extreme examples of this are suicide bombers whose CRSs have been implanted with a Driving Belief that says dying while killing the opposition is a great honor. Their behavior does not seem outrageous or unusual within the cultures that support it. This reality has become the accepted norm.

Thousands of beliefs hold lesser clout than Driving Beliefs. They seem less compelling and can sometimes be overridden by intention. Many are less fraught with emotion and are contained in more circumscribed themes. Those beliefs are secondary to Driving Beliefs. "I am an adult and I make my own choices" can override the belief "Sweets are bad for you." With full intention, you choose your favorite dessert. Just as some ARs are never deleterious, all Driving Beliefs do not run us amuck.

Louise tells a story about a drive across country years before highway rest stops and air-conditioned cars. Her father was quite eccentric. His underwear of choice was a one-piece BVD suit with a button-up front and a rear-access hatch. During the journey, he washed several suits in a motel sink. However, they were not dry the next morning. He spread them over the luggage in the car trunk. Later in the day the family needed a break from the dry Kansas heat. Her father parked under a small tree beside a barbed wire fence. Since they were taking time to have a cold drink from the cooler, her father draped the BVDs across the fence for drying. Coincidentally, a few minutes into the rest period, a huge swarm of locusts came past. Everyone quickly jumped into the car and they went on their way.

When Louise's father later began to dress for an appointment, he discovered he had left his BVDs hanging on the fence about 75 miles back. He angrily gave Louise the car keys with instructions to return for his BVDs. When she and her sister reached the site, no underwear could be found. They returned and jokingly told their father that the locusts ate his BVDs. He did not view this as comical. Although he could be quite punitive, he had no grounds for chastisement. He himself had created the loss. Thirty-five years later, Louise and her sister break into peals of laughter whenever the words BVD or locusts are mentioned. Their CRS recorded one of the few times they were able to "get one over" on their father and go unpunished. It is an emotionally charged event, but they have no desire to erase this imprint because it brings such pleasure when triggered.

An ingrained Driving Belief is the result of perceptions and emotional responses which occur when we are compelled to accept something as reality. This is notably true in regard to the self. As you might expect, those beliefs that are cloaked in stronger emotions have greater clout. There is reason for this. Usually, those beliefs have been instilled by repeated modeling, along with fervent and sometimes impulsive passion. Parents and/or SOs, in their own fear, blame and shame, drive home those beliefs which they feel, believe and perceive must be personal laws. Some of these laws become Driving Beliefs for the targeted. We see this in religious fervor to the point of war. Generally there is little rationale for these personal laws. A parent feels helpless, wants to feel in control, and becomes abusive. A mother feels stuck or unfulfilled and pushes her daughter to become what she was not privileged to become. A father longed to play ball but was coerced into staying on the farm, and now expects his son to do the same. A teenager wants to become an actor but that profession is seen as sinful by religious stepparents. Driving Beliefs can generate over- or underachievement. One lady says, "I was physically exhausted and felt I could not keep going. Yet I showed up. A friend asked, 'Don't you ever think of taking a bit of time off?' That had never occurred to me."[11]

The examples given barely touch the surface of the many types and expanse of Driving Beliefs. Believing that you will behave differently "this time" when operating upon a Driving Belief is a disaster in the making. We cannot quarantine a belief. Driving Beliefs can actually set a life course, especially those that are singular in focus or related to purpose and intention. For example, a mother dies for her child. A relentless CEO refuses to take no as an answer from anyone because he cannot allow himself to fail. An employee saying no might threaten his own purpose. Driving Beliefs can exist in direct relation to role assignment by SOs in our lives. Since the CRS holds these roles as truth, our reality is that we must play out the role.

But I am ahead of myself. That discussion, like the last stages of the third trimester of pregnancy, will eventually appear. For now, remember that personal laws established as Driving Beliefs are central to our reality and function. They can cause us to maintain plateaus of behavior. Differentiate between beliefs and other stories you hold as truth. "I believe I am going to get that promotion" can be mistaken for conscious hope with little, supportive data. Driving Beliefs are different than saying, "I believe I'll go shopping." A true Driving Belief creates a degree of fervor, and at some level, prompts or urges a defined behavior or aspect of who you are. Like the IRS, it will not be easily denied.

Fundamentals

A Driving Belief is a concept that the subconscious holds as a truth which must be impelled into action in the presence of a previously defined set of circumstances.

Irma believes she must be peaceful, loving and kind to everyone. She is, as evidenced by her behaviors and as validated by her friends. She inherited (learned) a strong work ethic and often ties this with her proclamations. "I'm working as hard as I know how to be peaceful, loving and kind." At work she says, "I'm working as hard as I know how to do a good job at work." When speaking of her mother, she says, "I'm working as hard as I know how to love my mom just the way she is."

When planning a vacation with friends, Irma was asked whether other family members might also be invited. She preferred that some not be invited because recent travel with them was tedious and angering. Everyone on the conference call burst into laughter as Irma painstakingly said, "I'm working as hard as I know how to *not* make it hard."

Irma's conscious mind was attempting to override her "be kind to everyone" belief. She was taught that whatever she tackled must take hard work whether it was eating monosodium glutamate, taking dictation or hunting garden slugs. This created a Driving Belief of "I must do the right thing." The truth: Irma was tired of working hard to prove that she loves certain people. She just wanted to go have fun on her vacation.

Even Luke Skywalker might have occasionally wanted a bit of downtime.

Thinking We Are Directing the Show Don't Make It So: Subconscious Imprints Usually Win

The Director of Nursing Education (DNE) intensely chastised my use of humor, then declared, "Other students were laughing *at* you, not *with* you, and it's disruptive."

I spent a couple of hours crying as I walked the streets. I asked classmates if her comments were true. Not one person verified her truth, but I could not speak freely, make humorous comments, or laugh without restraint for weeks. I now understand that I used humor to ease the discomfort I felt at being in that school. The DNE apparently failed to see that motive. Her assault imprinted my Cellular Response System with, "You do not fit in. Better watch out; you don't know who to trust."

I had admired this woman to the point of mirroring some of her professional behavior. Now I felt her authoritative intensity. I was blindsided, *thinking* I had no recourse, *thinking* I had been betrayed and belittled. For years, I exercised caution in the presence of those who outranked me. I won awards, yet was never certain I could simply be myself. What a waste. I could have saved a lot of tears and kept a bit of sanity by just starting a rumor that the DNE was sleeping with the hospital Chief of Staff. I guess wisdom *does* come with age.

Auto-Reactions are always given priority over conscious choice. This has scientific basis. Guyton, in his classic *Textbook of Medical Physiology* shows that punishment and fear can literally take precedence over pleasure and reward. Most people will never dissect a brain to see what manual stimulation of the cortex can do. So let's look at a real-life example.

The CEO issues a directive, "Everyone is to be present for a meeting at 7:30 p.m. today." Reading the memo, you have a sinking feeling. Last month you finagled tickets for tonight's Big Concert as a surprise anniversary gift. Your spouse idolizes the lead singer. It is a one-night only show. You are in line for a promotion. What a conundrum. You sit wondering whether your stomach will hold its contents as your body courses through various emotions. Do you choose work or the concert? You have just entered the twilight zone of Auto-Reaction.

Fear is likely to be present because you must choose between your work and your spouse. For some that would not be difficult. For most, angst will occur. If your decision arrives in the presence of heightened emotions which push your choice, you can be fairly certain that the CRS has been triggered.

We routinely face dilemmas because impassioned emotions so often accompany CRS imprints. Have you ever experienced a gut sensation when the smell of a certain perfume or food wafted past your nostrils? All senses, details, wit, wisdom or ignorance related to a specific event can, in a flash, gush into your being. Your physical body can go limp or stiffen, dependent upon whether the aroused memory is one of getting lost while spelunking or making passionate love.

All this happens in a millisecond without conscious thought. Interestingly, when we make a conscious effort to relive a particular moment, the recall is not as poignant or as explicit as it is when an AR occurs. In these urgent flashes, the entire scene of the imprinted episode can be instantaneously experienced and can include both the familiar and some previously unrecognized bits of that slice of life. Whether the original incident was pleasant or unpleasant makes no difference. During that moment, strong emotions caused you to react. Dr. Candace Pert, pioneering researcher in mind-body medicine, puts it this way.

> "What we experience as an emotion or feeling is also a mechanism for activating a particular neuronal circuit—*simultaneously throughout the brain and body*—which generates a behavior involving the whole creature, with all the necessary physiological changes that behavior would require."[6]

If this circuitry experiences conflict and the event gets recorded, the emotions of that life story now live in your CRS. Similar circumstances—odors, sounds, words, etc.—can recreate the same sensation. We have a sense of this. You never again want to smell a fragrance associated with your ex-spouse. You never want to envision the first time you got totally drunk. I feared using humor and felt "butterflies" when in the presence of higher ranking nurses. Whatever our perception was at the time of the imprint determines how we now respond to similar circumstances.

Shirley declined the invitation to the office party. Persistent appeals did not budge her. When the truth was revealed, fear was the culprit. Shirley's automobile had been broadsided when making a left turn out of the office parking lot. For two years, she had turned right out of the parking lot, made a left turn at the first traffic light, and so forth, until she came full circle. If she followed another car to the party, she would have to make a left turn out of the parking lot. Rather than face the potential of a second accident, Shirley chose to miss the party. She very much wanted to go, but her CRS had recorded an emotional zinger. Her ARs directed her to forevermore avoid turning left onto that thoroughfare, so as to circumvent the physical and emotional pain of another accident.

Obviously I have chosen an extreme example. How else would I make my point? Few high achievers would duplicate Shirley's behavior. Our conscious directives and rational thinking would compose the odds, knowing that we would be safe unless we were reckless or nonobservant. The example, however, demonstrates the power that emotional imprints and ARs can have in our lives. The CRS is constantly tapping into our environment. Television commercials are an example of how others can connect with our subconscious. They are filled with suggestions and professed maxims. Ad designers are super adept at tapping into our beliefs regarding having the best, the latest, the most unique, the "necessary" or what everyone else has. We perceive that they are correct, based on our own beliefs, and away we go to purchase the cough medicine that is state of the art, or the pain reliever that works the fastest. The item may or may not be what your unique body needs. Frankly, turning off the TV makes my headache go away.

Neuropeptides, a bodywide system, carry emotions into almost every cell of the body. These cells "learn" and retain "memory" of emotional experiences. Candace Pert's research revolutionized our thinking about emotions. She states, "Just as drugs can affect what we remember, neuropeptides (the carriers of emotions in the CRS) can act . . . to shape our memories as we are forming them, and put us back in the same frame of mind when we need to retrieve them."[7] So big deal. What does that have to do with performance and achievement? About as much as paint had to do with Van Gogh's masterpieces.

Dr. Pert's findings have complex and extensive relevance to performance. When we pursue a goal which is in opposition to the information residing in the neuropeptides—or in *Beyond Best* language, the Cellular Response System—that information is retrieved to automatically avert the conflicting input, thus affecting our choices and behavior. Dr. Pert gives an example. "The other day, my husband suddenly realized why he has had an irrational hatred of bluejays all his life. As a seven-year-old, he had painted a bluejay model in a confined place with a foul-smelling paint that had made him vomit. . ."[8]

"Suppose you have decided to take a fun motorcycle ride. Just before leaving, you open a letter from the IRS saying they are auditing your return. This feels like harassment since you were audited last year. The auditor was a pain in the butt, and you felt as if you were in the hot seat during the entire process. You remember your dad's repeated IRS-related conniptions and the resulting "Nobody buys anything 'til I pay those SOBs and get them out of my hair. I don't owe, but I still have to pay—(expletives)!" Now, you believe (because of programming in the CRS) that you, too, will likely suffer financial loss." In this picture, there is a genuine possibility that you might be so preoccupied with your internal dialogue about the IRS that you fail to see an oncoming car and cream your Harley."

Welcome to Waterloo. In this situation, your fate would be akin to Briggs and Stratton setting up a mowing contest near a mudslide. A personal coach could not guide you more precisely toward unmindful riding. Forget the attorneys. Reprogram your CRS and save your money. Besides, the IRS letter was actually addressed to your neighbor. In your haste, you opened it by mistake. Do you see how emotions can flood you?

Many high achievers prefer to leave emotions out of the picture, particularly when focusing on performance and career. The bottom line is that because Auto-Reactions take priority over conscious choice, this is an impossible task. Even when you think you are leaving your emotions at the curb, any condition that triggers the CRS will thrust you into an Auto-Reaction faster than Clark Kent can switch to his cape. Issues of the past continually fashion our performance. Simply put, emotions can override rational thought. Understanding this concept is of utmost importance for anyone desiring to go *Beyond Best*.

Fundamentals

Auto-Reactions are always given priority over conscious choice because they are recorded concurrently with an incident that is aflame with emotion.

Agnes rode her bicycle to the Peace Vigil. Smiles and good wishes abounded. She and a few others decided to ride bicycles through the intersection, ringing their bells. As she waited for the traffic light, a policeman approached and said, "Ma'am, you can't ride back and forth through that intersection."

AR Time! Agnes's face reddened. "I came straight through 'cause I didn't wanna make a left turn on Erie." She knew he was right, but she wanted to add fanfare to the vigil. Her desire for peace was forgotten when he asked, "Are you with this group?"

Agnes testily answered, "I'm going home! I'm turning right on Erie. I live on Erie. Agnes believes no one has the right to tell her what to do. In a flash, she gave an answer that supported her perceived right to ignore the officer. They argued. Finally he said, "Okay. You can go. But be careful."

After he left, Agnes said to bystanders, "I don't give a flying ____ whether he wants me to go or not! He can't keep me off the road. I have a helmet and lights and I pay taxes. I'm legal!" She swore as she pedaled off into the darkness.

Agnes's intention was and is that peace prevail, but her CRS held a program that instantly eradicated her peaceful state in the presence of an authority figure who challenged her. The goal of peace fell into the abyss of police authority.

I wonder what would have happened if someone had begun singing, "Let there be peace on earth and let it begin in me"?

7 Beliefs and Behavior Paradigms Govern Us: So What the Heck Is a Performance Set-Point?

YES! I WANTED A NEW VAN. A FRIEND AND I WENT INTO THE dealer's showroom. The salesman ignored me, waited until my younger friend approached, turned to her and asked, "May I help you?" If a photographer had been near, real money could have been made by capturing my friend's face as she exclaimed, "You'd better talk to her. She's the one with money." The salesman's perceptions totally miscalculated the situation. My friend, based on her perceptions, took offense, thinking that he had pegged me as a "little ol' white-haired lady." (Friends come to your defense in the strangest ways and oddest moments.)

As we continued, the salesman talked down to me and ignored my requests to order the exact van I wanted. He insisted that he had *the* car for me already on his lot. His intention was to sell a car. No attention was given to rapport. Ultimately, I went to another dealer. This man was fortunate that I was excited. Otherwise, my Auto-Reaction might have reared itself. I have a few programs which, when triggered, can cause others to call upon their emergency evacuation rehearsals.

Each of us has an internal directory of comfort zones. They include performance, integrity, guilt, vulnerability, fear, responsibility, success quotas, wealth and innumerable other areas. These comfort zones define our paradigms of behavior. We may ignore them, forget them or have no conscious awareness whatsoever of their existence. Still, they are there. For instance, I am fully aware of my fundamental limits in water ballet since I barely swim. When seated in a fine restaurant, looking over a scrumptious dessert tray, I may know my limits but ignore them. On the other hand, I have limits associated with certain fears which I have never realized. If I had to cliff dive in a life-or-death situation, I have no idea how much anxiety I could or would tolerate.

Auto-Reactions help maintain the various comfort zones.

The Cellular Response System catalogues the information which sets the boundaries of our comfort zones. Thus it is driven to monitor our behaviors and needs. Auto-Reactions help maintain the various comfort zones. We tend to feel highly charged issues most quickly and intensely. Others are subtle or go unnoticed. This is an important distinction because there can be a conglomerate of interrelated beliefs which have a tendency to propel each other.

Arnold saw two men standing in front of his new luxury convertible, one with his foot on the bumper. He angrily yelled, "Get your foot off my car! What the hell do you think you're doing?" The men looked surprised, but obeyed as one of them said, "Gezzz! What the heck is his problem?" Arnold is a kind man and would not have been rude in other situations. But he had saved scrupulously for quite a while to get this particular car. He kept it immaculately clean and clear of clutter.

Six months earlier, his brother's new car had been stolen from the spot where Arnold's car was now parked. It was never recovered. His father was a tyrant about his automobiles and had strict rules with clear punishment, no eating or drinking in the car, no rough housing, no feet on the upholstery. On the day mentioned, Arnold had been laid off from his job. Here there was no single isolated belief that caused Arnold to angrily demand that the guy take his foot off of his new car. Several interrelated beliefs were grouped together. Each had its own emotional charge and each had other interrelated beliefs with which they were coupled.

Demands, conformity, obedience, stress, potential damage to his prized possession, his father's old rules, a previously stolen vehicle, loss of income, and many other beliefs, emotions and perceptions were a part of Arnold's reaction. When he saw a shoe resting on the bumper of his new convertible, this collective network spontaneously auto-reacted. In that flash, Arnold became a territorial governor. For those few moments, Buddha, himself, accompanied by a chorus of oms would have had difficulty shifting Arnold's anger.

Everyone has an accumulated variety of Driving Beliefs that jointly govern performance, achievement or other behaviors. These closely associated webs of emotions and beliefs, come together to form behavior paradigms. After awhile, they collectively begin to indisputably shape ours lives. As the paradigms develop and govern our responses, these accumulated behaviors form a subconscious network which compels us. We establish actual Set-Points related to emotional and performance agenda as this network is laid down. They systematically determine the level, quality, extent and timing of performance.

"Stay out of that street or I'll whop you," the associated emotions, perceptions about authority, and other input can create complex beliefs. This humorous example might result in, "I can never cross the street except at an intersection. I must look both ways. I must be careful, and I can move forward only when the little white man is walking."

Numerous Set-Points exist concurrently. Whether opera or country music is revered or tolerated is determined by perceptions, experience, emotions and physical feelings. So is the determination to exercise, to be a computer-geek or an Elvis impersonator. A parent's compulsive behaviors with money combined with thwarted desires might produce manipulation. This Set-Point could permit scheming with a clear conscious because of believing I have the "right" to have what I desire. The same situation in another could produce a Set-Point that causes them to go to great lengths to avoid being manipulated. Set-Points are extraordinarily complex and precisely individualistic. Never disregard their existence or lessen their importance. Most, in some fashion, have an interrelationship to going *Beyond Best*.

Performance is a key issue in human pursuit. Check out any ice hockey game or observe a local politician as he or she dishes out mustard and pickles at a fund-raising affair. Nicole Kidman could take acting lessons from those guys. Performance, from total inability (think Oprah repairing a computerized car motor) to paramount performance such as Lance Armstrong in the Tour de France, is directed by Driving Beliefs and controlled by Set-Points. Lance himself has said, "It's not about the bicycle."

Just as a metabolic Set-Point controls an individual's weight, Performance Set-Points determine your level of success and how you go about getting there. Personal Set-Points, just like the metabolic threshold, are set internally and are not controlled by conscious thinking or intellectual directives. They stem from a web of unresolved emotional issues, embedded beliefs, perceptions, internalized directives, and paradigm thinking. Since they are held in the cellular structure they cannot be seen or dissected, but they absolutely exist. Metabolic Set-Points function automatically. Performance Set-Points do the same.* The terrific news is

* Performance here refers to any act, achievement, conduct, work, function, production, posturing, maneuvering, undertaking, discharge of duty, practice, proficiency, skill or any other personification of an individual be it physical mental or emotional.

that either can be altered. Thank goodness, otherwise some of us would still be obsessed with dial telephones and typewriter erasers.

Performance Set-Points govern success, proficiency, failure and conduct just as automatically and tenaciously as the metabolic Set-Point controls body metabolism. Through them we maintain specific behaviors, values, principles, rules and individual roles. This is the reason I, along with Bruce Lipton, Candace Pert and other scientists can so emphatically state that our perceptions control our lives. The predictability is notable.

A young man wants to be an actor. He yearns to be on stage full time and, in fact, has proven in semi-professional performances that he is outstanding in ability and talent. The next step is to move to New York. He deeply loves and honors his parents. He also knows that they need him in the family grocery store. He faces a career decision. Some imprinted beliefs are triggered. His conscious mind may list the pros and cons of leaving or staying to work in the store. He could just as readily be headed for the Falkland Islands to become a camel saddle salesman. His perceptions and Set-Points, not his career are the basic issue.

The ultimate decision will be related the comfort zone of this man's Performance Set-Points. Any emotional issues associated with leaving his parents in a lurch, following his passion, being a responsible son, being an out-of-work actor in a strange city, money, siblings and so forth can take precedence over his conscious thinking. The paradigms of behavior contained within his Performance Set-Points carry the majority of weight in his evaluation process. The decision he ultimately makes may take a little longer than deciding what to do if he were facing a grizzly bear on a hiking trail. Nevertheless, the restrictions this man will experience while making this decision are just as automatic and every bit as life-threatening or life-enhancing.

Lest the reader think that Set-Points are just bellyaching annoyances that inhibit progress, let me assure you that they are also vital to our emotional equilibrium. If they did not exist, we could get in over our heads. We also might never be motivated to achieve at high levels or in different capacities. We could make an even greater spectacle of ourselves at the annual pie eating contest, or be inclined to tell a policeman precisely what we think of his speeding ticket. Our behavior paradigms would be dramatically different, our lives more radical and less maintained. Without Set-Points, our performance, responses and productivity would be erratic. It is likely that personal pain, discord and universal pandemonium could prevail. Even though they hamper us at times, Set-Points provide behavioral boundaries which can offer direction and prevent persistent chaos.

Logic might lead us to think that Auto-Reactions and Performance Set-Points put us into a Catch-22. This can be true when conflict is present. However, angst can be eased since as we rewire the Cellular Response System everything shifts. Systems Theory demonstrates that any part of a system, when altered, affects all other parts of the system. As beliefs are shifted, ARs are lessened in number, and the conscious mind is more capable of observation and input. Changing a single Auto-Reaction can significantly alter performance efficiency. When we eliminate a Set-Point, we hit a kingpin, and, in so doing, open a peak performance gold mine.

What if Todd Beamer had had an Auto-Reaction that said, "Take care of yourself, buddy. No one else will," or "They have guns. I'd better sit still and listen up." We can only speculate what he might have done or said instead of courageously planning his move and giving the now famous "let's roll" command. The terminus of Flight 93 on 9/11/01 could have been very different.

Fundamentals

As a result of an accumulated variety of behavior paradigms that govern our responses, we have a web of emotional and performance Set-Points which exist at the cellular level.

Dennis was a building contractor with social skills and charisma. Contracts came easily. His business grew. Things could not have been better. His company and personal accounts were lush.

Dennis loved building his company. Wining, dining and carousing with women were also high on his priorities list. Giving money to the IRS was low. His CRS was wired for pleasure at any cost. His wife's request for a divorce hit hard. He had failed to keep any honor whatsoever with her. In retaliation, she reported his tax payment "negligence." Dennis lost his home, his wife, his children, his company, his car, his income, his financial reserve and, worst of all, his self-respect.

Dennis's father was alcoholic. Sometimes he "brought home the bacon" and sometimes not. His mother was demanding, selfish and martyred. Dennis's childhood was basically sacrificed to his parents' demands for responsibility beyond his years. When, as an adult, he was free, he reverted to the behavior he had witnessed during his formative years.

Dennis's behavioral paradigms undermined and ultimately destroyed his success. Had he learned to engage more with family, to drink less alcohol and to have fewer extracurricular activities with women, who knows what might have happened?

Dennis's set-points permitted cheating, excess drinking, diddling women and hokum, but his wife and the IRS did not.

8 If It's Not One Thing Controlling You: It's Something Bigger

WHEN I WAS STUDYING FOR A GRADUATE DEGREE, it was common knowledge that Dr. Lacy, treated me differently than the other students. I did what I was asked to do, but seemed to do the "wrong" thing or come up short. Once, Dr. Lacy was pushing me farther than I wanted to go. I honestly explained some difficulties, keenly aware of being in a lesser position of authority. Dr. Lacy asked, "Is it me, the head of the program, or me, the person?"

My engrossed conscious brain went through every thought I could muster, desperately thinking, "It's the program. It's you, the program." If a brain can hurt due to intensity of thinking, mine was certainly painful. My very being was excruciatingly filled with the struggle of saying the "right" thing vs. saying what I felt. Yet out of my mouth came the words, "It's not the program. It's you, the person." A single one of those proverbial feathers could have put me solidly on the floor. I absolutely *wanted* to say the opposite. I actually feared saying what I said because of potential repercussions. Still, the words I struggled to avoid came spilling across my lips.

During the previous year, a number of my contextual personal laws had been repeatedly piqued by this woman. I was tired of her pushy, passive-aggressive and punitive behavior. I believed I did not deserve to be singled out in this way. My response had little to do with Dr. Lacy and everything to do with my subconscious hardwiring. She could have been the caretaker for Stonehenge or a Guardian Angel for Michael Jackson. It would not have mattered, because one of my Set-Points had automatically done its assigned job.

Generally, a single Auto-Reaction is unlikely to cause a radical performance or behavior problem. If, as a child, you stepped on a green snake and experienced curiosity without condemnation, ridicule or punishment, chances are, in adulthood, green snakes would never alarm you. Conversely, suppose that your mother yelled hysterically and insisted that someone immediately kill the snake. As an adult, your response at seeing a snake would likely be reactive rather than curious. Your perceptions, colored by your emotions, would establish how you now behave.

Compare the following stories. Robert was an only child whose mother protected him from his father who consistently belittled him. Robert, according to his father, was irresponsible. Mother was happy to have her precious little boy all to herself. It took her attention away from the troubled marriage. Robert repeatedly looked to his mother for answers and comforting words. Mom's hug solved many problems.

Simon was extremely athletic. His mother doted on him and his brother. She attended Little League games, baked cookies for school functions and ran interference for her boys. But she also consistently had angry outbursts and blamed them for things gone wrong. She made unreasonable demands. Her rules were numerous and strictly upheld. In moments of passion, it seemed her motto was, "Somebody's gotta be blamed and humiliated and it ain't gonna be me."

As you read about these two men you already know aspects of their adult behavior. Your perceptions cause you to have mental responses to each situation. Your personal beliefs affected your mental assessment. Yes, Robert still is intensely connected to his mother. As she grows older and less independent, he spends long periods of time with her, calls her almost daily, and goes to her if anything is wrong. As for Simon, he calls his mother periodically, sends flowers on special days, and visits as he can.

Both men had dedicated mothers, but personal laws which drive their current devotion are quite different. No single issue created this. Simon had a goal to "get outta here" because of unbending rules and intense emotional hits. He hated his mother's rage. He hated the guilt he felt. He hated the anticipation of an accident or some wrongdoing being discovered. He learned to be "on guard" with his mother even though he loves her. His devotion is keener to his wife and children. However, he is one of those, shall we say, "henpecked mates." Beliefs regarding his "rights and privileges" affect his work performance. He tends to abuse company privileges, and brags about what he will and will not do. However, in private, as most "henpecked" husbands do, he cowers or leaves the scene. Obviously, his Auto-Reactions do not complement high achievement. Simon probably will never become the head honcho, unless of course, he is commander in chief of the doghouse

Robert's mother's protection fed a belief that he was special while also giving him an ally. Like Simon, he learned to hide but in a different way. He takes painstakingly good care of himself and disregards how his "specialness" affects others. In the workplace, Robert gets along with his peers but has difficulty carrying his share of the workload. If the situation feels too overbearing, he simply quits the job, knowing that his mother will help him until he "gets on his feet again." Robert, like Simon also will never be the big cheese, but for entirely different reasons. Instead of a doghouse he, who rivals Morris—the world's most finicky cat—will be too busy dreaming of a design for his perfect castle in the sky.

Are you concluding that this discussion has turned into a commercial for psychoanalytical thinking? Do you think that such data is about as important as learning the lotus position for a business meeting with Condoleezza Rice? As useful as a Tupperware party at the New York Stock Exchange? Hang in. The situations described may seem far removed from yours, but each of us has our own explicitly designed programs. Looking at the processes of others can foster self-analysis.

Looking at the processes of others can foster self-analysis.

Let's go for a down-to-earth visualization which may be helpful in my less-than-erotic postulate. Imagine a flat board eight inches square which contains 50 small, headless nails. The nails are only partially driven into the board and have been haphazardly set. About 200 rubber bands are hooked over the nails in various ways. Some attach from one nail to another, others cover three or four nails, some two, some six or seven, others wrap around 20 or more. No order or criterion exists for the bands. They may be of any size; short: long, medium, wide, narrow, thick or thin. Certain bands are interwoven above and below others, as well as overlapping those nearby. Interspersed among the nails are a few large, headed nails extending above the headless nails. These king-pin nails serve as a "hitching post" for large numbers of bands that are stretched and woven throughout the neighboring network.

Although oversimplified, this visualization serves as a metaphorical representation of the Cellular Response System. The board, along with all the nails and rubber bands, collectively represents our subconscious hardwiring. The nails, where clustered, represent a community of involved cells. The network of rubber bands symbolizes beliefs, unresolved emotional issues and internalized directives housed within and among our cellular structure. There is a weblike arrangement created by the rubber bands as they overlap, interweave, parallel and interconnect. Let's agree that they can only be removed with a particular solvent (reprogramming).

The CRS holds our imprints just as the board holds the nails. In the metaphor, the kingpins represent our Set-Points. Several Auto-Reactions (rubber bands) are "hitched" to or contained within a Set-Point. These headed nails are the pivotal points for the majority of the bands in a particular network. Set-Points hold the tension for a number of imprints and become a pivotal influence for the Auto-Reactions clustered around a distinguishable theme. One of Simon's Set-Points might include the theme of authority-associated rebellion, fear, paralyzed will and dread related to verbal badgering. Whereas, an authority connected Set-Point for Robert might have an underlying theme of being dutiful, staying out of the way, performance anxiety, and the need for allies.

Just as a kingpin in the board governs the bands connected to it, a Set-Point governs Auto-Reactions associated with it. Removing the kingpin totally changes the tension in all bands connected to it. Likewise, resolution of a Set-Point totally changes the "tension" which engages its Auto-Reactions. This permits a person to raise the bar on performance, setting the stage for going *Beyond Best*.

A large number of Auto-Reactions control a Set-Point. This is, in part, because our beliefs and perceptions around specific issues accumulate and intensify as more and more emotional data and beliefs are added. *When that data remains unchanged*, the older we become, the greater the number of surrounding beliefs related to each contextual law. This can account for at least some of your continued bitterness about your bachelor Uncle-who-did-me-wrong Ned. Complete behavioral paradigms may be integrated to comprise a Set-Point. An example would be that of beliefs based in religious dictates. Set-Points can also seem to take on a life of their own. President Nixon demonstrated this. His Set-Points apparently gave him free reign to use presidential power to approve crime in order to achieve his goal of being reelected. In the end, this was his demise.

As many degrees exist along the Set-Point continuum as there are people. Some compel one person to defy odds that would precipitate insanity in another. I knew a woman who had a single assignment at her job in the local hospital. She made Jell-O every day for 26 years. You might say her Performance Set-Point was locked on "steady as she goes." Okay, we need Jell-O makers just as we need brussels sprouts processors and CEOs. Count me out as a stirrer, though.

Lest the reader think that Set-Points only bring difficulty, here is an example that demonstrates how they also compel behaviors that create and support goals. When I returned to school at age 45 to become a chiropractor, I felt overwhelmed, especially in relation to my antiquiated study habits. I had to again learn how, when and what to study, and how to connect with teachers in a way that supported my efforts. I abhorred sitting through exam after exam of multiple-choice questions. Give me an essay question and I'm fine. I can give you a book!

In the early semesters, I wanted to quit and considered doing so several times. A Set-Point both disallowed quitting and increased my determination. Had that Set-Point not been in my CRS, it is probable that I would have discontinued my chiropractic education. I'm very glad to have had it because some very wonderful, satisfying and meaningful experiences have come as a result of being a holistic doctor. Yet, as I have grown in wisdom and knowledge, I also know that eliminating that Set-Point could also be beneficial. Sometimes it makes good sense to quit and travel in a different direction. If you give up stirring Jell-O, you might discover that making chewing gum is a joyful thing.

Fundamentals

Several Auto-Reactions may control a Set-Point.

Jana loves animals. She protects them, rescues them, has several pets, and exalts those associations that promote noncruelty to animals. She had pets as a child and loved them deeply. However, her attachment to each animal was short-lived.

Every time the family went on vacation, Jana's pets, especially her dogs, were euthanized. Her parents did not want to trouble friends with pet-sitting responsibilities or to pay to have them boarded. Had this happened once or twice over a period of time, Jana may have been able to resolve her emotional response to what she viewed as outrageous cruelty. But it did not happen a few times. Every dog she acquired was given the same treatment. To Jana, this was inhumane behavior.

In addition to her emotional attachment to animals, Jana has some negative feeling associated with vacations. She also works tirelessly in a paramedical position and regards her patients as her personal responsibility. Her performance at work, at home and with friends is colored by her plethora of personal laws which urge caringtaking, never taking time off, and refusing vacations.

You might say that instead of going to the dogs, she has given her life to the dogs. (Groan!)

9 Snared Stories Can Get 'Cha

Every experience does not create a reactive program in the Cellular Response System. If this were true, we would be so loaded with Auto-Reactions and Set-Points that there would be little time to consciously use our intellect or develop our talents. Some of you think a few people are unable to use their intellect anyway. Nevertheless, it is true that perception is based in personal history. When a person emotionally responds to a political or religious meeting, a speech, an accident or a helpless child, that individual has history which consciously or unconsciously relates to the current experience.

During the president's State of the Union address, those whose beliefs align with his, applaud. Those whose beliefs are in disagreement withhold applause, indicating disapproval. In either case individual perceptions determine the side with which they align. Occasionally the entire group will be in agreement and the president gets a standing ovation. Alas, some of those tricky bills still do not make it through congress.

The input that establishes the legislators' beliefs is more varied than the stripes on a herd of zebras. Personal concern over stopping a tax proposal may not be the main force behind disagreement. There is often an emotional connection to proposed bills because of the potential impact passage would have on their personal life or, perhaps, on their wallet. That senator is not engaged in an Auto-Reaction. Attachment to the outcome is because of a *perception* that there is a lot to lose and much to gain.

Every personal story does not create ARs or Set-Points. However, the source of every Set-Point is a story. Whether the story (experience/event) creates a Set-Point is dependent upon three factors:

- The intensity or emotional reality of the experience
- Whether the CRS is imprinted, i.e., the extent of the engagement in the body's physiology through neuropeptides
- Whether the individual is able in some way, to resolve any conflict that arises.

If your brother shanghaied and broke your Nintendo and you walloped him without getting caught, it is unlikely that your CRS recorded a program based on that incident (story). However, if you walloped your brother, got caught, took a parental whipping, and your brother badgered you with persistent gloating, as you continued to seethe, you could easily have imprinted the CRS.

Mary worshiped her brother. She loved waiting for him to come home. Tim would hug her as he slipped her a surprise. He was Mary's knight in shining armor. He played with her, protected her, encouraged her, went to bat for her, taught her about life and loved her sincerely. Tim was a sibling, a surrogate father, a playmate and Mary's hero. When he was drafted into the army, Mary was heartbroken. She thought Tim had abandoned her. Tim returned but was married and moved elsewhere. Mary missed him terribly until she got married.

Thirty-five years later, Mary was divorced. Months later Mary continued to be depressed, weepy, unsettled, frightened and lonely. In the past she won awards for her work performance. Now she had difficulty accomplishing assigned responsibilities. Mary's reaction seemed excessive. She could not understand her behavior since she was glad to be freed from the abusive marriage.

Mary's *perception* as a child, her story, was that she had been abandoned. With assistance, she now saw how that story presently affected her. Just as her brother left her, the man whom she had deeply loved and honored was now gone.

Here, all three Set-Point factors of a life story were replicated: emotional intensity, physiological responses through her neuropeptides and the inability to resolve her conflict. When Tim left, Mary's pain was too intense, her vulnerability too profound, her loss too overwhelming. She was emotionally paralyzed. When, in the present time, a similar set of circumstances came into her life, all the original emotional turmoil was replayed by Mary's CRS. Her reactions had nothing to do with her husband, per se. She knew she needed to get out of the marriage. Her subconscious still carried the emotionally laden story of perceived abandonment by Tim. Those same emotions were again piqued.

Neither Mary, the child of the past, nor Mary, the adult, had the ability to keep a very important man in her life. Her response, then and now, was uncontrollable by logic, intellect or willpower. As long as he was around, Mary, like Tammy Wynette, stood by her man. But, when abandonment (absence of her man) became the issue, when she was again alone, her ARs overrode her will. Like Mary the child, Mary the adult could not control her loss. Neither remarrying nor a heart transplant was needed. Setting Mary's story free from the neuropeptides that snared it brought relief.

A significant detail in Mary's story is that she was completely unaware of the reasons behind her extreme reaction to living without her husband. (As tedious as spouses seem at times, many helpmates miss 'em when they are gone.) Rationally, Mary knew that it was good to be rid of the rascal. However, since she was in an Auto-Reaction, understanding was outside her cognitive awareness. Had Mary not resolved her story, those same ARs, like the Ghost of Christmas Past, would return if she experienced such a loss again. Set-Points are like the Green Hulk. You do not want to keep bumping up against them.

There are times when stories (significant events) are not consciously remembered and times when emotions may not be overt. Some events can be buried in the subconscious, inaccessible to easy recall. Still, if CRS physiology and neuropeptides were engaged without resolution, they affect our perceptions. The imprints remain connected to the original story.

Just as all stories do not generate Auto-Reactions, all memories cannot be trusted for accuracy. Dr. David Neubauer in a posted comment, March 2006, states:

> "When we try to recover an experience, our minds don't simply forget some details and leave corresponding blank spots in our memory. We have a tendency to fill in gaps with invented details that seem to make sense. Clear but partial memories become mixed in our minds with other associations and details. We don't remember things the way a video recorder documents events, from beginning to end... We reconstruct the events... Psychologists who study memory have known for years that it is possible to create extremely vivid memories of events that did not actually occur. Lawyers know that eyewitness testimony is remarkably unreliable."[9]

This means our CRS programs are, at times, based on stories that are less than factual. We hold a grudge about mama's nurturing when she did nothing to merit our animosity. She was just a lousy cook. We couple inaccurate memories with our concepts of reward and punishment. Guyton points out that almost everything we do is related in some way to reward and punishment. These centers constitute one of the most important of all the controls of our bodily activities, drives, aversions and motivations. Punishment and fear can take precedence over pleasure and reward. This, in part, accounts for the fact that perceptions affect our reality.

A number of people have written about Emotional Reality—what we *perceive* to be true. I like the concept as presented by Dr. Scott Walker who says: "Emotional Reality and Historical Reality can be, and sometimes are, identical. However, they can be quite different. Both realities are based upon the *perception* (emphasis mine) of the individual's physical, emotional, mental and spiritual state at the time of the experience."[10] Dr. Walker goes on to say that the vulnerability of the mind-body system determines whether or not an event is recorded as a pattern. In other words, we may accurately or inaccurately record stories in our CRS or not record a pattern at all. Since punishment and fear can override pleasure and reward, and vulnerability determines whether a pattern is recorded, you can see that imprints of our stories and perceptions provide thousands upon thousands of opportunities for subconscious programming. The surprising thing is that most of us avoid being mental patients. Perhaps children need an annual pilgrimage to Lake Titicaca where they could confer with the extraterrestrials on matters such as how to more rationally and favorably manage the adventures of childhood.

Mary's feeling of being abandoned was her Emotional Reality. To the CRS, Emotional Reality is no different than cognitive reality. When Mary divorced, she became as vulnerable as when Tim left for the war. Her Emotional Reality was the same in both experiences because each event had the same underlying story. When Auto-Reactions kick in, talking about "what's wrong," repeating declarations, attempting to "fix," blame or get even does little more than increase vulnerability and raise our blood pressure, or create a need for a Personal Chaos Headquarters.

When have your emotions rather than common sense or sharp intellect compelled you? Did you secretly read confidential files or take credit for contributing to a group project when you had barely participated? Our stories drive us. James was headed for the top. However, he began to have difficulty getting work completed on time because he was striving to do everything perfectly. There is nothing wrong with having perfection in mind when completing a task. The problem was James's CRS definition of perfect.

In the sixth grade, James wrote about his favorite vacation. He proudly shared it with his father who excelled in English. He ridiculed James's writing and told him his grammar was terrible. In his vulnerable state, James made a vow to "get it right" without his father's help. His CRS was set to push him toward the impossible—perfection in writing.

James's new promotion brought more freestyle writing. Subconsciously, he was still trying to prove that his father was wrong about his abilities. Vulnerabilities regarding being ridiculed, inept and less than bright were affecting his performance. Although he definitely was not a Radio City Rockette, James would have needed little coaching had he been one. His own relentless pursuit of perfection would have driven his performance there or anywhere else. A vulnerable 11-year-old boy created impossible standards for operating in an unrelenting, very real adult world.

Be aware. Our CRS-imprinted stories can cause us to take up residence on Fantasy Island and have us think we are Thurgood Marshall, when in fact, we are acting more like Judge Judy.

Fundamentals

The source of every Set-Point is a story, although every story does not elicit a Set-Point.

Louise's parents attended church almost every time the doors opened. As teenagers, she and her sister did not want to spend their time sitting in a church pew. They looked for ways to entertain themselves during the service.

One game was called "The Sheets." They took turns locating song titles in the hymnal to which they could add the words "In Between the Sheets." The person that found the funniest songs was the winner. For example, "Love Lifted Me" became "Love Lifted Me in Between the Sheets." "Oh Holy Night" became "Oh Holy Night in Between the Sheets." It was not unusual for their stifled giggles to provoke admonishment from a parent. Once, their giggles were not sufficiently suppressed. This resulted in severe punishment. Both wailed, wept and became angry, but it did not stop their game. Their private pact was to keep the game going no matter what, and creatively plan new strategies to surreptitiously play it.

Here punishment and increased restriction (emotional issue) became an empowerment. As adults, Louise and her sister occasionally laugh long and loudly when recalling this memory. They especially enjoy telling the ways in which they tricked their parents as they try to catch their breath between peals of laughter.

This is a story that did not elicit a Set-Point. Their vulnerability was lessened by each other and their alliance against their father. Like Caesar, they came, they saw, they conquered. But, most of all, they had fun.

10

Auto-reactions Commingle: Is That What You Want?

WHEN A NUMBER OF COMPLEMENTARY AUTO-Reactions and Set-Points collectively come together, a paradigm of behavior is formed. There is no particular reason for a specific behavior paradigm. There is no single Set-Point that drives a person. It is not a matter of locating and eliminating one performance Set-Point or Auto-Reaction and then you are then home free. There is a tremendous overlapping, tangling and crisscrossing of our imprints. The Cellular Response System is a virtual web of programs, each waiting for the appropriate stimulus that awakens it.

Various aspects of life drive the types and depth of paradigms we develop. For example, how we perceive and respond to SOs sets at least some of our beliefs about power, and authority. We hear things like: You wouldn't know the difference between a rock and hard candy. Big boys don't cry. Dummy, what do you know? How could you be so stupid? Eating spinach makes you stronger. These or similar words of wisdom can define a personal power which might equal a deep sleep.

A father who models power through stringent rules and arbitrary punishment may have children who exhibit similar behaviors. This same father may have a child who decides, empathically, that S/he will never abuse another person. A mother who is an enabling martyr is teaching her children overt powerlessness, although her children have the opportunity to learn the art of manipulation. Some take on the challenge of being exceptionally "powerful" to insure that no one will ever "walk" on them. Some become so compliant that their lives never take personalized form. A child takes from the parent that which best suits their immediate needs. These imprints shape behaviors throughout life even though needs change.

Why is it that people have completely different reactions to the same stimuli? Why does one child become a "teetotaler" while a sibling screams, "Yee-HA! Bring on the Party"? This question may be, in some ways, rhetorical. However, we do know that Emotional Reality, especially during childhood, plays a large role. During that time we have no individual authority, per se, yet in some ways it is every man for himself. To be a "successful" child, one must run the gamut of all the personalities in their life and come up with viable options of adaptation which permit individual progression and being. In many ways, adulthood is the same. Each person's Emotional Reality is pivotal in the work world, personal life and private moments.

Behavioral paradigms usually are not fundamentally taught. They are slowly built as we take in, personalize and reinforce who we think we are or should be. Auto-Reactions and Set-Points accumulate, and our behavioral patterns are crystallized. The way we perceive our environment determines which stories and directives we buy into. The subsequent paradigms determine and regulate our concepts and activities. Obviously, we also have the ability to make conscious choices about our behavior, performance and life's journey. The problem is this. As we pursue goals or climb the rungs of that proverbial Ladder of Success, a lack of understanding of our behavioral paradigms or ARs can strangle efforts and obliterate opportunities. Everyone, from graveyard maintenance people and Jaguar nameplate inspectors to Fortune 500 CEOs, has this potential liability.

Cheri Huber wrote a book entitled *How You Do Anything Is How You Do Everything*. Of course! Your behavioral paradigms mandate it. A friend once told me, "The only thing you have never been successful at is quitting." Friends have a wonderful way of jolting you when it's needed. My imprints compell me to explore or do the next thing—and my list is long. Yet, when I left my practice, within a year I was again working two to three days per week, without advertising or doing any recruiting.

In today's changing world, outdated paradigms of behavior often no longer sustain performance. There is a new world paradigm into which we must fit. Lifestyle can be built around achievement and advancement to the point that personal and family life is consumed or put aside. Some discover they have high achievement but are on a treadmill going nowhere. The harder they work, the faster they run, the longer it seems to take to reach the top. Along the way, certain beliefs take a backseat while others catapult to the forefront. Technology and massive information can overwhelm paradigms whose designs are insufficient to meet the challenge.

Some discover they have high achievement but are on a treadmill going nowhere.

Ideals may be sacrificed. I am a classic example. As a chiropractic intern, I adamantly opposed the required patient x-rays. My song-in-residence was, "When I have my own practice I will never take x-rays! Radiation is dangerous." My strong beliefs regarding holistic care and what I *perceived* thrust aside the opinions of others. Soon, though, I was practicing in the real world, with real situations and the accompanying personal responsibility and liability. It took a very short time for me to crank up the x-ray machine.

Vickie Sullivan of Sullivan Speaker Services says, "It's real easy to bet the farm when you don't have one." When you have assets and increased responsibilities, and have become an economic engine for a number of people, you feel you must continue in your achievement. The difference between those who sustain success in a changing environment and those who cannot is often an inability to change their preexisting paradigms. In my own situation, I had to shift some of my beliefs. Otherwise, I would have jeopardized people's lives. My conscience and my practice would have suffered greatly. I would have gone down the tubes faster than a circus fat lady on a schoolyard teetertotter.

A story will demonstrate what can happen when paradigms persist and nothing is done to change them. Eva had the following Auto-Reactions:

- Passive-agressive anger if she did not get her way.
- Working hard to "prove" that she was responsible.
- Helping others was a mandate.
- Getting something for herself by controlling the situation.
- Could not overtly receive.

These Auto-Reactions were set as a child. Her anger stems from her father's demanding rules. His way was *the* way. Over and over, Eva's plans were spoiled. "Responsible" behavior was rewarded, but he defined "responsible." As a surgeon, he believed, "If a patient calls, a *good* doctor goes." She learned that helping others took priority. Later, as a nurse, Eva followed her father's example. By helping others, she, herself, would somehow be rewarded. (Subconsciously.)

Since mother was the buffer for father, Eva felt compelled to stay in her mother's good graces. In addition, her mother depended on Eva for her own emotional support. (Where was the Parenting Patrol?) Eva's reward for this role was secretive permissions and closeted gifts. Her mother was her ally. Child Eva translated this into, "I must not disappoint or I'll have nobody." She acted "responsibly" so as not to get into hot water, while learning to covertly control situations to her benefit.

Eva became a martyred, constantly scheduled-to-serve, controlling woman who, in passive-aggressive anger, can clip your wings as she smiles and says, "I love you." Only she can "do it right" and therefore is overburdened. In the doctor's office, Eva outworks other employees. (A good nurse and daughter takes care of everything.) She wants to be in the know (controlling behavior). She tells others how hard she is working and that she also has a heavy workload outside the office. (See how good I am?) If someone suggests she lighten her load, delegate or relinquish outside commitments, she smiles, explaining why only she can do certain things. (She must remain loyal and she must control the situation.) Through her smile she responds, "I wish someone else could." (See how important I am?) This paradigm has become Eva's truth, and it mercilessly drives her.

Human behavior is extremely complex, in part because our cell receptors constantly and consistently analyze the environment to uphold our beliefs. One slight difference in the environment or our perception can create a dramatically different outcome. In one situation a single belief may be consciously overridden or ignored, whereas in a different situation it would stand supreme. My belief that eating sugar negatively affects health is held in a behavior paradigm regarding food and health. It is a very strong belief based upon my education and experience as a doctor. I have upheld that belief consistently both in my practice and my personal life. But, in the ice cream store, my conscious mind says, "So what? I'll have a double dip of pineapple-coconut, please."

Defusing emotional charges of original unresolved events will reset behavioral paradigms just as it does with ARs and Set-Points. Do not confuse *thinking* you have changed a paradigm with actual reprogramming. Changing a paradigm requires active elimination of existing beliefs. As long as a paradigm remains constant, the related behavior will continue unmediated. Behavioral paradigms can be beneficial or your worst enemy. General Motors represents a corporate example of this. It has been the world's largest automaker and global industry sales leader for 75 years. In years past, U. S. presidents would fly to Detroit, give a talk and, thus, set the economic policy for a year. Not long ago, GM decided to maintain status quo. They kept their existing operating paradigm. Recently, when the presidents of the Big Three wanted an audience with President Bush, it took about a year to get it. In December 2006, the Washington Post printed Toyota's announcement that it is on track to become the world's largest automaker in 2007, thus dethroning General Motors once-pivotal place in America's economy and politics. There will always be a high achiever nipping at *your* heels. Modification of behavioral paradigms is, at times, expedient.

Fundamentals

Complementary Auto-Reactions commingle to create paradigms of behavior.

A shepherd was tending his sheep in rural Wyoming. A new Jeep Grand Cherokee screeched to a halt next to him. A young man in a Brioni suit, Cerruti shoes, Ray-Ban sunglasses, Jovial Swiss wristwatch, and a YSL tie jumped out and said, "If I guess how many sheep you have, will you give me one of them?"

The shepherd looked at the man, looked at the sprawling herd and said, "Okay."

The man connected his wireless modem, entered a NASA site, scanned the ground using GPS, and opened a database and 60 Excel tables filled with algorithms. He printed a 150-page report on his miniprinter then turned to the shepherd and said "You have exactly 1,586 sheep."

The shepherd answered "Say, you are right. Pick out a sheep." The young man took an animal and put it in the back of his vehicle. The herder looked at him and asked "Now, if I guess your profession, will you pay me back in kind?"

The young man answered "Sure."

The shepherd immediately said, "You are a consultant."

"Exactly! How did you know?"

"Very simple," replied the shepherd. "First, you came here without being invited. Second, you charged me a fee to tell me something I already knew. Third, you do not understand anything about my business. Now, I'd really like to have my dog back."*

*Taken from the Internet.

11 Did You Know? Subconscious Barometers Determine Your Future

We continually amass information in the Cellular Response System. Much like a web that continues to build, both old and new information comprise Driving Beliefs and governing Set-Points. When old data is not cleared, the subconscious matrix becomes inordinately complex.

A fifth-grade girl experiences difficulty with spelling and her teacher does not help her understand spelling rules. In high school that same girl is expected to spell correctly and no help is forthcoming. Eventually she comes to believe, "I can't spell." She squeaks through college English composition. A simple situation becomes shrouded with emotion. Groundwork is laid for yet another Set-Point.

Just as ARs can form Set-Points, the latter can come together to form a subconscious performance barometer. This network regulates the amount, type and urgency of behavior. The young woman will consistently add CRS data when confronted with spelling. She is not an empty-headed bimbo who must be relegated to becoming a binocular distributor or a balloon broker. She qualifies for election as President of the United States! Yet, she is definitely held back in one area of her life.

As information is added to the network, we get hooked. Harold loves basketball. He is constantly on the court at school, in the park, or anywhere he sees a hoop. His parents require certain class grades, otherwise he is not permitted to play. Harold is at odds with the math teacher. The teacher's attitude annoys him. He also knows this "stupid math class" can keep him from playing ball. After awhile, this becomes a self-fulfilling prophecy, and Harold's basketball time is suspended. He then becomes hostile toward his parents and resents their authority to keep him from his beloved game. The scene has been set. Harold believes he is stupid in math and becomes hostile when authorities direct his life.

In high school, Harold wins a place as starting guard. Algebra is a mandatory class. By now he has bought into the notion that he cannot do math. He becomes "dumb" in Algebra because of the unresolved emotional trauma at age nine. Harold is now old enough to make broader decisions. Still, his love for basketball and his coveted starting position seem far more important than algebra. His CRS barometer, along with his acceptance of being "dumb in math," places him in a predicament. The struggle with algebra precipitates old hostilities which affects his game. His performance means he is not always in a starting position. He hates math. He hates his teacher. He hates being second string on the team. Harold is cornered. Fear and anger overtake him. Looking for a way out of his dilemma, he begins cheating on his math homework and tests. The cheating causes Harold to feel guilty.

Harold's Set-Points continued to expand as he hits the same pattern again and again. At the university, math classes will present the same challenge to Harold *whether or not* he is playing basketball. There may be automatic self-deprecation, anger and, perhaps, cheating. One trauma was networked with another and another. In the presence of this performance barometer, Harold may be stymied in situations where he feels inept. When pursuing something he loves, it is likely that something will happen to block him. At work, he may fail at a particular aspect of his assignment or may work surreptitiously to get around them. Fire walking with Anthony Robbins, or a miracle from God could change his performance. In the meantime, he remains vulnerable in particular areas, and his subconscious will set off the same chain of events. The details change but the dynamics remain the same.

Our subconscious barometers maintain performance boundaries. (To some of you that is about as interesting as listening to the sounds of a crawling caterpillar, without video. Stay tuned.) Some aspect of our personality is accommodated by these boundaries. A flash of anger feels great in the moment. "Showing them" can bring buoyant relief. We experience this brief comfort, but often have remorse afterward.

There were assumptions on top of assumptions in Harold's plight. He falsely assumed that the teacher knew how to teach—well, maybe he didn't go that far! He and his parents assumed nothing could be done; the teacher was right, he would never be able to learn math; math was more important than basketball (Duh! Not to Harold.); restrictions would coerce him into studying harder; studying harder meant Harold would learn math; and, on and on. Anywhere along this line of assumptions, there could have been an intervention. Something as simple as a tutor might have accomplished what everyone wanted. As it was, Harold became so inflamed with reactive emotions, he laid down personal laws that would haunt him later.

Blair Singer points out that leading edge thinking in business today is that psychological stress, emotional upset, and past incidents are a detriment to success. Those experiences, he says, can reduce efficiency and productivity. If they can be eliminated then there is the possibility of having a whole new level of productivity. Being able to function in the present is the single and most powerful edge any business or individual will have. "At that point of clarity, the future can then be viewed without obstruction from the past."[12]

No single belief or incident creates a performance barometer. One horrible parent-teacher conference about a spitball contest in the fourth grade will not undermine your chances of becoming an aerospace engineer. The *network* of complementary CRS imprints establishes the barometers which compel our internal paradigms. They determine our perception and, thus, dictate our principles, roles and responses. The primary focus, therefore, must be that of uncovering the subconscious fiends that bridle you so that they may be defused. Chances of performing antithetically in their presence are about as great as seeing a staunch pacifist piloting a B-2 Stealth bomber. You may as well try to propel a lawnmower with coconut oil.

If you are programmed for performance perfection, you will spend longer hours and extend greater effort at work, whereas someone else may go home early. If you are washing the family car, it must be immaculate; another merely rinses off the mud. All your reports must be in perfect order. Your unwritten personal laws drive you to perfection in every task. If placed in a situation which disallows your model of perfection, you will have difficulty. You may experience anxiety. If a supervisor wants greater production without regard to ideals or excellence, you may feel as though you are in a glass pressure cooker. As a perfectionist, you cannot accept mediocrity. It makes no difference whether you are advising the CEO or learning to be a sword swallower.

When someone is wed to success through Set-Point barometers, the more complex, sophisticated and intense their tasks become, the more likely they are to sustain success. Conversely, the "also-rans" are driven to success only to the point at which their performance barometer stops them cold. Yet another who is wed to achievement, but lacks self-worth, may go into a vicious cycle of putting out personal fires which are ignited by continued bumping against performance Set-Points.

When Nathan retired, he started a consultation service. However, the behaviors that served him as a Fortune 500-company executive became his downfall in the private arena. Clients were happy to have the job completed, pay his fee and send him on his way, but Nathan would linger. "I'll just do this and I won't charge you." His CRS network demanded companionship which overruled common sense, intellect and observational skills. After-hours marathon sessions were welcomed in his previous employ, but to the small business person, Nathan's persistence was as welcome as Linus on the pitcher's mound.

Signs that the body-mind is in conflict with the conscious mind include, but are not limited to:

- Emotional reactions such as persistent anxiety or shut-down
- Unwanted patterns of behavior that persist.
- Vague apprehension or angst.
- Fruitless efforts to change no matter what you do.

Other responses can range from mild agitation to fear, guilt, blame or shame, along with varying degrees of immobility or depression. This does not mean that you are incapable. It does mean that it is time to go on a CRS scavenger hunt. New cognitive solutions or passionate affirmations will not change the situation. The CRS can hold you hostage. My friend is a shopaholic and clothes fanatic. She recently sold her bed in order to have floor space for a new wardrobe. Now she has a whole new problem. The couch is not as comfortable as she thought it would be.

Fundamentals

A performance Set-Point serves as a subconscious barometer that controls precisely the amount or type of performance you may obtain.

Julia worked as a dispatch officer. She liked the work, management was pleased, the drivers were friendly and the pay decent, but in a few short months, trouble was brewing. When someone needed overtime, Julia would oblige. If bad weather caused a backlog, Julia handled it. The boss could safely leave Julia in charge. She had learned to create a plan that pleased the drivers while economically safeguarding the company. She listened to drivers' problems. She managed to rearrange itineraries without ruffling feathers.

Julia took care of others at her own expense, feeling she was needed. She ignored her own needs when others were in crisis. Personal law demanded that she keep peace, do her best and serve without anger. The drivers saw her pattern straightaway, and many used this knowledge to their own advantage.

In two strenuous years, Julia was burned out. She could no longer physically meet the increasing demands or absorb being constantly riddled with guilt at not being able to "do it all". There was no way for Julia to win. If she were promoted to a more responsible, higher-paying position, it is probable that her ARs would eventually precipitate physical illness.

Julia needed a little more of Miss Piggy's style and presence. "I always knew that I was destined for *le top!*" She attributes her rapid rise to: beauty, talent, wit, intelligence and modesty. And she expects a lot of assistance and loyalty from others.

12

A Performance Plateau Is The Subconscious Saying, "No More"

A LARGE FIRM HIRED RHONDA, SOON AFTER SHE RECEIVED her degree. She enjoyed apprenticing with seasoned professionals, but wanted her own practice. After learning the ropes and stashing money for start-up expenses, Rhonda took the big step. She was in high spirits, but those energies were short-lived. Nothing had prepared Rhonda for the dog-eat-dog world of competing for business, nor the constant effort to build a client base. Skilled, bright performers sometimes look more at what they want and less at investigating how to get it, or assessing personal tools needed to accomplish the goal. Sometimes the picture on the cereal box is given more value than its contents.

Rhonda believes she has the right to do things her way. She also believes that "*they* do it to her" without just cause. Therefore, anger and resentment, instead of data and logic, guided some of her decisions. She put the appropriate pieces together for a successful solo enterprise, but she overlooked vital personal behavior paradigms which would defeat her.

When something went awry, Rhonda found someone to blame: the printer, the government, the landlord or anyone within her thinking.

There is little room for blame and anger in the presence of clients. Yes, Frank Sinatra, we do have the right to do it our way, but sometimes our way is not the most efficient or rewarding way. The beliefs that created Rhonda's longing for self-employment were the same beliefs that made having a private business difficult. In a Biblical story, Ruth says, "Whither thou goest, I will go; and where thou lodgest, I will lodge." Beliefs are the same.

When we attempt to go beyond our personal laws, biochemical, structural and emotional aspects of the Cellular Response System come together to collectively say, "Stop." Therein is the making of a Performance Plateau. Rhonda's barometer said, "You may go no farther with this. Letting 'them do it to you' is in opposition to your rules of conduct (beliefs)." She reached a Performance Plateau, intellect and hard work notwithstanding.

There is a concept called serial ordering of events. Simplified, it means that we can list, in order, any series of events. Then, by interrupting that order, a different result will occur. In other words, "Do something different. Get something different." Shifting a Performance Plateau is similar. As long as Rhonda persists in routinely recreating the Battle of Atlanta, we know her "Waterloo" is just down Peachtree Street.

When we hit a Performance Plateau, we generally resist the required activities that will move us forward. The CRS drives us to maintain behaviors that support our perceived roles. In the matter of business professionalism and service, Rhonda's perceived roles took her into waters over her head. She became excellent bait for proverbial and actual business sharks. If an AR in every instance says, "It's not my fault," then there is no way to shift from a downhill course to one of success. Blaming others for a business demise is about as relevant to success as environmental impact statements are to a pork rind.

Plateaus in performance can be scary. The desire is present. An opportunity may exist. Others believe in you. You know that you are capable. Yet you seem to make one blunder after another. Good fortune appears not to be on your side. Efforts seem redundant. Circumstances change. Options disappear. Contingencies appear. You find yourself in a predicament that overrides good intentions. Prospects change their minds at the last minute. You work harder to deliver more, but the sweet deal or promotion eludes you.

> *Sometimes Auto-Reactions prevent us from making desicions that are in our own best interest.*

Dogged determination, a plethora of staff, every conceivable electronic device (oops, that includes tapes), persuasive attorneys, and all the power of the United States presidency did not help Richard Nixon. In the long run, his habit of making certain that he got what he wanted stopped him cold. Most of us are not playing for such high stakes. Nevertheless, each of us has our own ultimate goal, desire or dream.

Sometimes Auto-Reactions prevent us from making decisions that are in our own best interest. Anita had progressed up the corporate ladder. It appeared she could do no wrong. Her ideas were innovative and timely. Her willingness to go the extra mile was obvious. A new CEO was hired and the rules changed. Whereas the previous CEO had trusted her and liked her ideas, the new CEO took nothing for granted in terms of loyalty. Anita had previously been given a wide berth and professional freedom. She dramatically resisted being bound to rules by a watchful eye.

New job assignments placed Anita in a position which cramped her resourceful and innovative style. At first, she extended her help carte blanche to the new CEO. But to her he felt like a man of steel, uncaring for the individual and focused entirely on the bottom line. Within weeks, she was transferred to yet another department where she was expected to develop a program which had failed attempts by four others. Anita's Auto-Reaction said, "You are being given the dirty jobs. He is trying to push you out." She brought the program alive, but to her dismay, it was then handed to someone who knew nothing about it because the CEO needed to laterally move another, less effective vice president. Anita was given a third assignment. Although she was extremely unhappy, she felt determined not to be pushed out, opting instead, to "leave when *I* make the decision and not when *they* do." Clearly her ARs were overriding her conscious assessment of her predicament.

Anita reflects a Performance Plateau of another sort. Her new work assignments were not the problem. Some people reach a plateau because of habitual behaviors. In this instance, change itself ignited Anita. She *perceived* that the new CEO was pushing her out when he restricted her. She wanted to keep her freedom and continue to be revered. Because of emotional responses, she was unable to adapt to the CEO directives. Emotions are the oxygen of Auto-Reactions. Anita's judgment, decision-making skills and performance were affected.

Anita's ARs kept her in an emotional struggle in the presence of new house rules. Instead of adapting, she became obstinate, paranoid and secretly defiant. Thus, she made decisions that negatively affected her success. This kept her tied to a rather dishonoring, if not ignoble, environment. One shift created havoc with Anita's career. She was stuck on a Performance Plateau that lasted for almost two years.

You might say the CEO was using Anita's talents. He may have given her "impossible" assignments knowing that she was capable. You could say, the CEO was oblivious to Anita's assignments because he was focused on a bigger picture. Only he knows. Here is a valuable point. Anita chose to continue her belief that she was being pushed out and shortchanged. Her downfall was her emotional attachment to not allowing that to happen.

The time to leave would have been when she felt the CEO was using her. Whether or not he was is immaterial. Either way, she was unhappy. Had she not hit a Set-Point, she could have said, "It really doesn't matter what he is doing. The point is, I'm miserable here. I don't like losing my freedom or being assigned the dirty work, so I'm leaving." But her emotional charges kept the Auto-Reactions coming. Perhaps Anita's paranoia was based in reality. Perhaps she created her own demise.

There are times for certain high achievers when success becomes a given rather than a goal. Sometimes they do not know whom to trust, who may be gunning for their job, who might be a Judas selling them out. What happens if you outperform the higher echelon? If you curtail your performance, you may be dismissed. If you overtake them, you feel disloyal. Many high achievers hit Performance Plateaus under such circumstances. Congruency can bring reprieve because you then have a different overview. Tarzan lived just fine in the jungle.

Fundamentals

A Performance Plateau is reached when a Performance Set-Point remains constant in the presence of conflicting cognitive will.

Jerri taught English although she held a degree in physical education. She needed work. Moving to another city was not an option because she felt responsible for her mother. Here, she was with her mother and the pay was good, but she desperately wanted to be teaching PE. For her, sports were the equivalent to blood transfusions. She could not stop thinking about doing what she dearly loved. Most of her conversations were about someday getting a job teaching PE.

Over time, there was less interest and preparation for the English classes. Jerri was basically going through the motions required by her job. The truth was that she and her mother probably would have had higher quality time together had Jerri commuted on weekends. Her CRS program, however, held that she be the caretaker and companion for her mother.

Eventually the disappointment, angst and discontent took its toll. Jerri became ill. Then she could not teach at all.

Why not let mama be free to find a companion her own age and go spread those PE wings in a nearby town? These options were ignored by both Jerri and her mother because of personal laws.

Mama needs reprogramming too. Pharaoh's soldiers got into big trouble when he changed his mind about letting the children of Israel go.

13 You Know Egos Can Stifle Greatness: What About Governors?

As a teenager, I had a pal whose foot was quite heavy on the accelerator. When he refused to change his driving habits, his mother had a governor installed on the engine. Ron could drive the car, but it would not travel more than 50 mph regardless of the force applied to the accelerator, how much gas was in the tank, or the posted speed limit. Likewise, an individual will not perform outside any context, move beyond a specific role or function differently than undergirding Set-Points permit. It is like obeying unwritten rules at your mother-in-law's home. Even though your conscious mind can think of no reason not to sample food from the pot, you instinctively know that you are much better off if you don't go there.

The CRS governs only when synonymous circumstances are encountered in current time. At midnight, your conscious mind says, "I'm hungry. I'll raid the refrigerator." As you pull out the rib roast, a voice says, "What are you doing?" Startled, you whirl around, and the rib roast goes flying across the floor. There is no time to consider what Julia Child would do. Before eyes can blink, you, in a single motion, snatch the roast and place it on the plate. You feel as if you have been caught in an illegal act. Logically, you know you will not be punished. Yet your heart pounds, your mouth is dry and your breathing has quickened. You then realize your daughter is laughing at the sight of roast beef skidding on the floor.

Why is your heart racing? Heart-Math researcher Dr. Rollin McCraty, among others, has shown that emotion is faster than thought. Somewhere, sometime in the past, it is probable that you were "caught" under a similar circumstance. Now, in a flash that puts Superman to shame, your body surges with emotion. The modus operandi is the same whether you are caught "stealing" food or attempting to push regulatory limits to gain a promotion at the office.

In *Good to Great*, Jim Collins demonstrated that great companies, by and large, were not in great industries. In no case was there a company that just happened to be sitting on the nose cone of a rocket when it took off. In over two-thirds of the cases, he noted the presence of a gargantuan personal ego that contributed to the demise or continued mediocrity of the company. He points out that greatness, rather than a function of circumstance, is largely a matter of conscious choice. For outstanding performance, the concept is not a goal to be the best, a strategy to be the best, an intention to be the best, a plan to be the best. It is an *understanding* of what you *can* be the best at. The distinction, Collins says, is absolutely crucial.[13] Whether looking at a company or ourselves, most of us never make that distinction. We tend to focus on competence that feeds the ego rather than uncovering what Collins calls our core competence.

I cannot overemphasize that the complexities of various Set-Points are far reaching as well as totally individualized. Even if twins suffered seemingly identical traumas, their Auto-Reactions will be different. John fails his bar exam. He is angry. However, he responsibly recognizes that he was lax in his preparation. He begins planning for how he will, *this* time, prepare for the bar exam. It is doubtful that this failure will greatly affect his performance as an attorney.

Don also fails his bar exam. He, too, is angry. To him, passing the board was a given. He accepted a job in a prominent law firm. The delay caused by failing the board will cost him the job. The crowning blow is that knowledge was not an issue. By some freak accident, Don failed to line up the answer sheet correctly on one page of the exam. Appeals and a hand check of the answer sheets may absolve the issue, but that takes too much time for Don. His practice of law may be dramatically affected, especially if he is forced to take a "leftover" position. His current success will depend upon the way he handles this setback, and his ability to resolve his anger without adding to existing CRS Set-Points.

Individuals who believe that fate has dealt them an unfair punch, or who live in a strong ego, sometimes shift to a stance of getting even. They function as if the end justifies the means. Conscious rationalization coupled with a strong ego can be amazingly intoxicating. Kurt Eichenwald in *Conspiracy of Fools* details Enron's internal battles over turf, greed and ideas as the company raced from one outrageous deal to another, consistently ignoring warning signals from analysts and accountants; all done with arrogance and compromised ethics.[14] Often these people stick out like a nudist colony in the middle of an airport terminal. Unfortunately, they have difficulty seeing that they are presumptuous and unscrupulous. This alone can prohibit anyone from moving *Beyond Best*.

Chance, in the movie *Being There* beautifully demonstrates purity of intention and congruent behavior. The other characters are oblivious to his simplicity, in part, because of their own persistent ARs and egos. In spite of being intellectually challenged, he appears capable to pull off amazing feats. In the end, he is seen to walk on water. He operated within the bounds of his core greatness, albeit, unwittingly. We can learn extraordinary lessons from satire and comedy because the truth is spoken or illuminated and allows us to examine ourselves.

Fundamentals

Performance Set-Points disallow performance beyond a certain level, within a particular context, or in stipulated circumstances.

Eddie, an Air Force pilot, had flown all over the world. Next, he flew for a major U. S. airline for 24 years. The airline went bankrupt. Finding employment was difficult because of his age and competition from other pilots in the same predicament. Eddie was proud and stubborn. He refused to work for less pay or to fly small aircraft because of reduced prestige. He took a job selling auto parts rather than "compromise his principles." Of course, he rather quickly quit that job. While he "lived by his principles" his family lived on his unemployment income, plus his wife's salary, for about three years. And she tolerated it! (Wifely duties Set-Points, I suppose.) His children saw a father who was unwilling to do all that he could to earn a livelihood.

This is clearly an individual whose Set-Points drove his performance. Eddie would not work in a "lesser position." Some judged and chided him. Friends attempted to help him and sometimes hounded him, but Eddie never understood the cost of feeding his egotistic Auto-Reaction. He never discovered whether piloting a small plane would be exciting, further utilize his training or bring a different outlook.

Can you imagine John Lennon or George Harrison refusing to sing without the other Beatles after they broke up their band?

Burning Desire With Belief Gets Us Zero Mileage Or Confusing Affirmations

Napoleon Hill said, "If the mind can conceive it and believe it, you can achieve it."[15] According to him this, coupled with burning desire, would bring your dream into reality. Many have interpreted Hill's comment to mean: if you think something often enough to convince yourself you believe it, then you can make it happen. However, repeatedly stating or thinking something does not always establish it within the subconscious where beliefs reside. Motivators and self-help gurus tell us to create and use affirmations. I advocate them in *Puppet or Puppeteer*, but neglecting to engage body physiology when using them is common. If you depend on affirmation alone, you may be left standing by your desk with IRS returns in hand, wondering, "How come . . . ?"

Dr. Lawrence Peter in his commonly accepted *Peter Principle* explains movement within a hierarchy. Basically, an individual is promoted to their highest level of competence, after which any further promotion raises them to a level at which they are or may become incompetent.[16] Before you decide to appoint me as president of the National Association of Fuzzy Logic, read on. The preceding chapters explain how we defeat our own achievement. Based on that data, we can assume that there are definite ways to avoid reaching our level of incompetence. President Clinton, well, you know that story. And then there's Martha Stewart.

When cognitive skills are in disharmony with governing Auto-Reactions, performance escalation cannot continue. The CRS will automatically deliver responses which negate progress. Consider the "King of Rock-and-Roll." Elvis Presley was an American idol. He had wealth, an almost unparalleled love affair with his audiences, a daughter he adored, a generous heart; and, he marshaled the attention of the world. With all his fame and fortune, he apparently died an unhappy man. One of his fervent desires was to become an actor who played legitimate roles in high-performance venues, what he often called "real movies." He knew that the movies in which he starred were mediocre—designed specifically to bring young admirers to the box office. He wanted to show the world that he had the talent to be a great actor. Elvis conceived that he could be a great actor and in his conscious mind believed it, but he never achieved it.

> The CRS will automatically deliver responses which negate progress.

Elvis tried in vain to realize his dream of serious acting. He repeatedly requested his manager to obtain serious movie roles for him. He consciously saw himself as capable of more demanding roles. Friends and associates encouraged him to persist in seeking those roles. He never created them. One might say Elvis's manager kept him from it. That may be partially true. However, one cannot overlook the fact that if Elvis had absolutely demanded he be given a trial run at serious acting, he probably would have been given the opportunity.

There is a scene in his life story (approved by the Presleys) in which

Elvis, as a soldier, wants to go home to his beloved ill mother. His manager said it was impossible. "You are in the army now. You can't just tell the army you want to go home!" Elvis's intense reply was, "Make it happen or you are fired." He went home. It was imperative for him to be by his mother's side when she was ill. That CRS program overrode everything else for Elvis. Why did he not command the same attentiveness to creating a role as a serious actor?

Elvis's fierce ARs with regard to authority figures was prominent throughout his life. A personal law also required that he keep his word, even in unseemly and nettlesome circumstances. How many young soldiers would, because of their promise, avoid having sex with a beautiful young woman who loved him ferociously? It appears that those ARs kept him stuck starring in movies he intensely disliked.

We can only guess at Elvis's Set-Points. His behavior in relation to his manager, though, was indicative of governing Set-Points which disallowed commanding, take-charge behavior in the presence of an assertive, sometimes overbearing, you've-gotta-do-it-my-way manager. Whenever Elvis approached him to discuss changing the direction of his career, that is, getting serious acting roles, his manager always overruled him.

Whether or not Elvis had the talent or skills to do what he so fervently wanted to do is unknown and immaterial here. His conscious desire and deep longing to experience and be seen as a competent professional actor were very real. So was his inability to consciously, clearly and directly command his manager to do his bidding. His supreme desire and his Cellular Response System functioned in opposition to each other. Therefore, he continued to make mediocre movies while his misery increased. The burning desire that Napoleon Hill spoke of resided in Elvis's conscious mind. He thought that he could become a consequential actor. He consciously "believed" that he could competently take on serious acting roles. However, he never changed those beliefs that compelled his behavior in the presence of authority. This is a classic example of how cerebral thinking and the ARs of the CRS can set up opposing compulsions that prevent progress. Elvis could order someone to arrange for a visit to his ill mother because his love for her overrode every other Set-Point. But he could not demand that the man who took authority over his career and his money get him serious acting roles. Burning desire and affirmations are not always enough.

Cerebral thinking and the ARs of the CRS can set up opposing compulsions that prevent progress.

It would appear, especially in Las Vegas, that Elvis is *still* trying to make it as a serious actor. Oops, actually those are impersonators *trying* to be as genuine as the "King."

Fundamentals

A Performance Plateau exists because Auto-Reactions housed in the performance Set-Point differ from conscious or stated goals.

Within weeks of joining the guild, Wallace was chairman of a committee, the new webmaster, and a cook for the annual picnic. Praise for his roasted pork abounded. The web site had never looked better, although postings were tardy. Wallace spread himself thin. His CRS said, "Serve."

The new guild president, in his perfectionistic zeal, (read must-do-it-right AR) sent letters to committees and board members: shape up or ship out. The guild is run by volunteers. When Wallace received a letter telling him of his ineptness as a webmaster, the proverbial "offal" hit the fan. After a public squabble, Wallace resigned from everything, including membership in the guild. He could no longer give service or be a part of any organization he felt did not appreciate him and his extended assistance and benevolence.

Because these men were operating from Auto-Reaction stances, everyone in the guild was a loser.

Business does not always come before pleasure; therefore, the ride might get bumpy. Sometimes boys will just be boys!

15

Wanna Stop It But Ya Can't? Yes, You Can!

Abraham Maslow's "Hierarchy of Needs" is accepted as a norm throughout the scientific world. A person's most basic needs such as food and shelter are at the bottom. These needs must be gratified and safeguarded before having concern about the need to belong. Basic emotional and belonging needs carry greater importance than self-esteem. Think of it this way. In the middle of a robbery, self-expression is likely to be absent. If I am falling from a burning rooftop, my mind, in that moment, has no brain cells devoted to self-actualization.

Gratification of needs is integrally related to Cellular Response System programming. After fulfillment of physiological needs, a person may seek safety and freedom from fear. This level is the stage where many Auto-Reactions are recorded in the CRS because each of us has a need for psychological, emotional and esteem safety. Early rules and regulations create one entry portal for fear. Sibling rivalry, fear of not being loved, fear of chastisement, separation anxiety or fear of being alone are but a few of the possibilities. The type and breadth of fears that may be instilled in a child are endless. Innumerable opportunities are presented for keenly charged emotional issues to go unresolved. A parent's rules and follow-through on the cleanliness of a child's bedroom can be smooth sailing in one family and disastrous in another.

We abide by our Auto-Reactions even if we totally disagree with them.

Tina provides a somewhat humorous example of a an Auto-Reaction created by a repetitious, emotionally charged event in childhood. She gets angry when her husband or children clip their nails in her presence. Tina's father was a demanding man with strict rules. Before going to bed, everyone gathered in the family room for a review of the day. Attendance was mandatory. If her father was displeased with someone's actions, as Tina puts it, "All hell would break loose." This also was a time when her father habitually groomed his nails. Tina's CRS associated "catching hell," rules and mandatory behavior with nail clipping.

In adulthood, one of Tina's reactive rules is that nails are groomed in private. This rule has nothing to do with her family's needs. Even though she now has the authority to leave the scene, Tina's CRS continues to respond as she did when she could not flee the family powwow. She agrees that her reaction is not always in her best interest. That's because *we abide by our Auto-Reactions even if we totally disagree with them.* I suggest that if, perchance, Tina happens to someday become a revered assistant you never want to lose, do *not* cut or clean your nails while she is taking dictation.

Since basic needs such as security and freedom from fear are paramount, we adapt our beliefs, responses and reactions to that which gives the greatest assurance of their fulfillment. Early environmental indoctrinations serve as "moorings" for equilibrium and safety and are of great concern. Rodney Dangerfield may have gotten "no respect from nobody," but he stayed around because his survival depended upon doing so. Survival and self-protection needs cause us to accept beliefs which alter our perception or cause unwanted behavior. How could getting hostile about your husband trimming his nails in your presence possibly support a loving marriage? It makes about as much sense as Sting avoiding microphones during a live concert.

As we grow to independent status, we have opportunities to evaluate our ARs and perceptions, but alas, there is no School For CRS Updating. There is no primer that teaches how to determine which beliefs promote our best interest. Amazon.com does not carry a book titled *Discarding Self-Defeating Childhood Beliefs for Dummies*. Thus our beliefs tend to remain with us unless our education, career, personal growth or life-changing event causes us to question them.

Generally, we do not give conscious thought to how we came to be who we are, or whether it is rational or beneficial to continue as that. We are pulled and pushed directionally and behaviorally. We automatically head in a particular trajectory instead of consciously choosing, even though this may not support our current viewpoint or provide the broadest satisfaction of needs. Those programs which are set in place as a means of fulfilling basic needs are extremely persistent.

Many individuals are highly successful *because* they have Auto-Reactions that drive them. They, too, may discover an imbalance. Others have ARs which permit or promote excellent performance but prompts them to operate "under the radar" or shun the spotlight. Still others are skilled performers and quite successful but downplay their achievements. Their Auto-Reaction is to disbelieve their own competence. Psychologists Clance and Imes identified the phenomenon of Imposter Syndrome.[17] Here, high achievers who do not believe in their own accomplishments are convinced that they are scamming everyone about their skills and abilities. No matter how successful they are, they continue to think they will eventually be uncovered as imposters. They are unwavering in their belief that they have somehow "accidentally" arrived. The reactive, skeptical internal judge can keep these people from taking risks in which they might excel.

It is well documented that we take care of basic needs in the same manner throughout life. "Good ol' boys" continue be "good ol' boys." Seducers continue to be seducers. Perfectionists continue to be perfectionists. Politicians continue to—I'll let you supply the end of that sentence. Situations change and performance demands vary, but reactions tend to remain the same. Early on, we learn to conciliate our basic needs. Later, when survival is not an immediate issue, the imprint is still in place. Behaviors such as excessive drinking or overeating in an attempt to drown the compulsion to achieve at all costs, losing one's self in competitive "play" such as golf or tennis, or working extremely long hours at the cost of family relationships may be the result of Auto-Reactions. If only the spouses and children knew this, routine family argument number 478 might be eliminated!

A country and western singer croons, "Baby, I *neeeed* you next to me." S/he is saying, "My basic need to be loved is fulfilled when you are at my side." Unfortunately, the two of them may be so engrossed in each other's company, frolicking along the turnpike of love and lust, that they become oblivious to heavy freeway traffic. No one thing, no one person, no one situation can satisfy our needs. Learning all you need to know in kindergarten is insufficient for the demands of a powerful career. Auto-Reactions that served a basic need at age three or four are unlikely the reactions that are needed as an adult in a thriving career. Paying attention to this fact may in itself reap an entirely different harvest for success.

Fundamentals

We abide by our Auto-Reactions even though we may totally disagree with them.

Soft spoken Eva grew up in the deep south. Cultural and parental indoctrination dictated that she show respect as well as respond to anyone older with "Yes, ma'am," "No, Ma'am," "Yes, sir," and "No, sir." If she erred, she must accept her punishment.

Eva was a loan officer in a small-town bank. All went well until, she got married. Her husband's career move took them to Detroit. Eva took a lateral transfer to a large, nationwide bank. The straightforward, blunt manner in which midwesterners spoke was a shock to Eva. Compounding the situation were peers and supervisors who were older. Her automatic responses of "Yes, Ma'am" and "No, sir" were perceived as impertinent. Her soft-spoken manner was seen as less than powerful. Instead of being known as respectful, she was seen as obsequious. Eva had difficulty holding her own because of cultural background and parental upbringing.

She wanted to fit in, earn respect and perform well, but repeatedly fell back into old patterns. Less ethical people could then take advantage of her good will and soft manner.

It is possible that some efficient army sergeant could help Eva override her CRS by effectively teaching her to say, "No, Ma'am! You are not permitted to stab me in the back, Ma'am. No, sir! I will not be your servant, sir!"

16

Resist or Accept: Your Cellular Response System Cares Not

When a conscious desire is congruent with Driving Beliefs and Set-Points, the resulting success can be stupendous. It is the difference between Charlie Brown and Dick Tracy. It is as though magic happens. Maria Schriver Schwarzenegger relates stories of childhood with her parents. Her father, Ambassador Sargent Schriver, organized and served as the first director of the Peace Corps. Her mother, Eunice (President Kennedy's sister), worked with mentally retarded children. Maria has followed her parents' model with her own impressive and extraordinary work as a successful national television journalist.

Maria speaks of family cohesiveness during her childhood years. Despite numerous worldwide responsibilities, her parents set aside time for the family to be together, to learn and to love. Daily, the question was asked, "What are you going to do for the world?" Those sessions literally programmed the children to contribute to mankind, to be responsible members of society. As they grew older and headed into the world of professions, business, politics, and heading their own families, they could embrace their hardwiring. High performance and success was a "built-in" expectation from early childhood.

Of course we do not know what goes on behind the closed doors of the California Republican governor's mansion, but my hunch is that since Maria comes from a staunchly Democratic family, a few burning Auto-Reactions might appear from time to time.

Auto-Reactions occur without regard to willing acceptance or conscious resistance.

What about conscious resistance to Auto-Reactions? Charlie Brown's very first failed attempt to kick a football occurred when Violet held the ball for him.[18] He was worried that he might accidentally kick Violet's hand and pulled away at the last second, saying, "I can't go through with it!" Later, Lucy reinforced his disgrace as she pulled the ball away just as he was about to kick it, saying, "I was afraid your shoes might be dirty." This fictitious character's unresolved emotional event kept him going back again and again for the same dream. Charlie Brown desperately wanted to kick the football. Lucy would say such things as, "I give you my bonded word," "You have to learn to be trusting," "Look at the innocence in my eyes," but always pulled the ball away. Chuck went back, year after year, *hoping* that the outcome would be different. He was programmed to keep going for his dream, *thinking* that his behavior would be different, *thinking* that this time he would kick the ball. Lucy was programmed to lure and trick him. She believed Charlie would willingly return again and again. Encoded Auto-Reactions kept them setting up the ball for failure for 48 years.

Auto-Reactions occur without regard to willing acceptance or conscious resistance. Maria Schriver accepted her program. Charli Brown continued to act as if his program was different than it was. You will know that your conscious directives and your Driving Beliefs are in opposition when:

- A particular pattern of behavior persists in the presence of conscious desires that are different.
- Changing a particular response seems impossible no matter what you do.
- Unexpected or seemingly inappropriate or disproportionate emotional reactions occur.
- You experience restlessness and boredom.
- Your Little Voice refuses to shut up!

Charlie Brown kept trying to kick that football even though he never succeeded, Linus profoundly believes the Great Pumpkin will come. Year after year, he foregoes trick-or-treat goodies to sit in the field and wait for the Great Pumpkin. If these comic strip characters were actual, live people, they would know on some level that Lucy would, once more, pull that football away and that the Great Pumpkin was never going to appear. However, they would also keep trying, just as they do in the comic strip, because of their beliefs and their CRS programming.

Spider-Man is programmed as a superhero. Darth Vader's programming as a villain was brought to the fore when he was angered about his wife's death. In the people world, Seinfeld is obviously programmed to bring laughter to humanity. In each, the CRS programs are in agreement with conscious goals and desires. That congruency enabled a full-fledged pursuit of mission with exemplary performances.

Fundamentals

Encoded Auto-Reactions occur in the presence of conscious resistance as well as in the presence of willing acceptance.

Ross Perot was an IBM salesman who founded Electronic Data Systems and turned it into a multibillion-dollar corporation. He is best known as the Reform Party Texan who ran for U. S. president. His short stature and big ears were ridiculed, but his folksy, straight-talking image won him 19% of the popular vote. He is labeled as obnoxious, controlling and ruthless, something most Americans did not see in his campaign.

Perot attempted to get out of the navy because he was shocked to see "godless, hard-drinking, carousing men" on his ship. He received awards and honors. However, he could not acknowledge his own dark side, the ruthless manner in which he fought his enemies. From external appearances, his Driving Beliefs say he is always morally right, and his motives pure. He must control every situation to fit these parameters.

The author of Perot's autobiography says, "These are his strengths and his weaknesses. They give him the independence and courage to envision huge endeavors and make the them happen... but they are so intense they literally threaten his sanity... Were he to achieve his goal of becoming president... he would surely become a heroic failure to rival anyone in Shakespeare or the Greek tragedies."[19]

We can only speculate. Still, since I have no direct protection connection with Superman, Batman or Spider-Man, if I am to deal with Ross Perot, I want him on my side!

17

Cajoling Gets You Nowhere: Whut Can Ya Do?

There is a common notion among us. If we learn more or do more, we can press beyond self-made boundaries. If we increase the number of hours in which we can push ourselves physically, a breakthrough will occur. If we "set our mind" to meet the challenge head on, and persevere, we will attain the goal. Any of these actions may aid our cause somewhat, but actual change in a performance Set-Point goes lacking. There are exceptional moments when someone decisively puts the past behind them and moves on. Genuine forgiveness fall into this category.

Dr Phil speaks of how he and his father argued incessantly. "One day," he said, "I decided I wasn't going to argue with him anymore." He let go of related unresolved emotional issues, and made an absolute decision. He did not *try* to never argue, he did not "set his mind" nor *think* he would no longer argue. He disconnected the hardwiring and set a new program. Dr. Phil reached deep into his subconscious self and made the necessary change to override an existing Auto-Reaction. Perhaps it came through forgiveness or some other emotional switch. The significant note is that his CRS accepted the new program.

A decision is an active resolution. Decisions incorporate choice, and the kinesthetic senses. By making a definite decision, we can choose to resolve a circumstance. I would take a bet that Dr. Phil disengaged some antagonistic emotions at the moment his decision was made. Observe this skilled professional, and you see that he intensely engages individuals so that kinesthetic involvement is obtained. Then, he drives home a new program. When, in the middle of an associated emotional fog, an "authority" tells you what you must do, the override can be quite effective.

Words alone do little to switch CRS imprints. Techniques such as repetitious writing, assertiveness training, positive habit training, positive affirmations or motivational talks will not remove a driving hardwired program. Some of the lesser agenda within the Set-Point network may shift. However, the more powerful, ingrained Set-Points must be addressed through the kinesthetic senses. Because of the associated emotions, the physiology of the CRS must be engaged. Tony Robbins attributes much of his success to reprogramming. If you have attended one of his events, you saw him engage as many senses as possible while "overwriting" with new information.

Kinesthetic experiences are involved in translating information into physical reality. A particular smell or a specific sound can elicit a flood of emotion. An emotional connection to an event can bring laughter or other physical responses. Your boss may cause a bad taste in your mouth. Our senses hold the imprints of highly charged emotional experiences, both positive and negative. In fact, Candace Pert has proven that our emotions regulate what we experience as reality.[20] Thus, engaging the kinesthetic senses in reprogramming the CRS is vital. Seeing and feeling a new program as you let go of binding experiences gives greater assurance that the link between the conscious mind and the subconscious is affected. Once the emotional charge is removed, there will be no Auto-Reaction. The wanted change in behavior can then occur.

Suppose Monday morning you awakened with the expectation of a great day at the office. Then you remember you had promised to return your friend's rare Beetle CD boxed set. But, two weeks ago you lost one of the CDs. How will you tell your friend? You begin to rehearse what you will say. Nothing seems proper. Next comes the self-punishment. *"Why did I lose that CD? What is wrong with me? How can I possibly tell him how stupid and careless I was? Blah, blah, blah."* Your emotions are engaged. As the day passes, you focus less and less on work because you are thinking about the CD. "Setting your mind" to ignore the missing CD is almost impossible. Trying harder will not change the feeling and reaction. Affirming that "It's okay," does not ease your angst.

Your program says, "I must not lose valuable property that belongs to others. I will be punished," and so forth. Because of your CRS imprint, each time you lose something of value or violate the trust of a friend, you will again go through frustrating self-talk and personal blame. Your performance barameter acts in the same way. You may do more, learn more, or direct yourself to "get over it," but you will not push past Performance Set-points by will-power alone. The Unresolved situation must be relieved of its emotional tension.

Sometimes we think we have made a decision or changed a program only to discover otherwise. Perhaps you think you will ignore your spouse's quips and innuendos regarding your hobby or certain friends. You may be successful for a month or so. Then suddenly, one day, you discover yourself rivaling Tarzan's call. There has been one wisecrack too many. Your internal Geiger Counter picked up the one subtle move that set off the CRS alarm. You are a screeching cheetah on a trampoline. Obviously, your "decision" to ignore your spouse's taunt was not a true decision. It may have been a conscious attempt to overrule an imprint, but the decision was not absolute. Your Auto-Reaction is as predictable as accidents on the Jersey Turnpike.

Fundamentals

Trying harder, learning more, "setting your mind" and other similar consciously orchestrated directives will not push you beyond a Performance Set-Point.

Oprah Winfrey with all her power, prestige, wealth, education, a private chef, the support of her life partner, and influential connections was unable to control the Auto-Reactions of overeating. She hired a personal trainer. She worked out daily. She ran a marathon. She repeatedly brought weight loss gurus to her show as she searched for the "right" diet. There were low carbs, restricted calories, hi protein-low fat, strict food portions, and restricted times for eating. She could not control her AR of: "I see potato chips, therefore I must eat."

Her trainer helped Oprah understand that the difficultly resided in her emotional responses. When she understood this and dealt with some subconscious issues, she established a program that works for her. The change is obvious not only in her weight but in her attitude and thoughts about eating. Her recent comment was, "I didn't know it was emotional. I just thought I loved potato chips!"

Many, many beliefs are contained in addiction Set-Points. Oprah may encounter other unresolved issues. Now, she will be better equipped to deal with them.

Do you ever wonder how many times Oprah had "The Last Supper" before learning that trying harder and learning more will not alter an Auto-Reaction?

18 Self Concepts Can Make You Miserable: Don't Be Who You Were Set Up To Be

Generally, our stories and adventures of life are experienced, enjoyed, forgiven, noted, or in some way settled, and we move to the next experience. Some events, however, leave behind a tug of war. Desire vs. compulsion, yearning vs. passionate devotion can persist. Overwhelming experience or having to obey the rules of others can become stories which turn into albatrosses. Whether or not we think they bother us or control our behavior, they continue to thrust their presence into our lives by influencing our perceptions.

If a woman thinks she needs a face-lift, depending upon the breadth and depth of her perception, she will have surgery, perhaps several, and even generate financial disaster to appease her perceptions. A man who perceives that all his conquests want prolonged sexual activity may carry a supply of Viagra, whereas the guy who perceives that safe sex is imperative may carry condoms. There. I did it. I brought sex into the discussion. Whew! That's done.

Unlike the CRS, the conscious mind does not always have easy access to all of our stories. Even when we remember, mental pictures and thoughts may provide no recall of accompanying emotions. However, those perceptions and emotions exist. As an amateur actress, I once played a hospice patient dying of cancer. She was blind and hostile. When anything she disliked happened, she mumbled, "Sons of bitches." That comment was so prolific in the script, that if I forgot a line, I only had to mumble, "Sons of bitches," and the play went forward without a hitch.

Some friends and I picked up the habit of using the phrase in real life. Being stuck behind a truck merits a "Sons of bitches." The ice cream store being out of a favorite flavor justifies a "Sons of bitches." Using a particular tone and making it humorous has created an inside joke. We have discovered, though, that whenever the phrase is used in the presence of others, someone in our group always explains how we have come to use that term. We *fear* others will think we are being rude or offensive. At times listeners do raise an eyebrow or act embarrassed. Without exception, though, we get a laugh when explanation is given. We mean no offense. To us, it can harmlessly turn a moment of tension into laughter. Somewhere in our CRS network, however, is a program that says, "These words are not permitted. Offensive. People will think you are disrespectful." Our perceptions, driven by fear, compels us to explain ourselves even though our intention is aboveboard.

Instead of responsibly, rationally or logically responding to current circumstances, perceptions draw our focus elsewhere and the stakes are raised. As a TV anchorperson would say, "I interrupt this paragraph to bring you an important message." Some level of fear, guilt, blame or shame are almost always present when the CRS has given an Auto-Reaction. These feelings can be masked by addictive or other sabotaging behavior. You can determine when a conflict exists by learning to tune in to your guilt, shame, blame or fear. This may take practice since they may be masked by years of inattention. The more subtle the feelings, the more practice you will need. Practice is merited because these four feelings are some of the most detrimental to progress.

Lucille decided to became a chiropractor. After receiving her license, she rented space, purchased equipment and informed people that she was available. There was an initial flurry of activity, but the bustle died down. A successful doctor offered suggestions for practice-building, but they were ignored because Lucille was caught in the blaming game. She wanted to serve. She liked being a doctor and had the necessary knowledge and skill. Other doctors in the practice were successful. Lucille, however, had never comprehended the intensity of her programming.

This woman is a consummate introvert. She did not do the leg-work and grunt work of building a practice. In six months, her practice folded. Three years later she is still blaming the other doctors and staff. "They 'took' everybody that came through the door." The telephone calls that *should* have been hers were given away. "*They* fouled up my appointments." Yul Brenner in *The King and I* would say, "Et cetera, et cetera, et cetera." Blaming is easier than looking at one's own behavior. Lucille sabotaged herself then used blame as ointment for the wound of failure. She was as doomed to fail as Wylie coyote is when chasing the Road Runner.

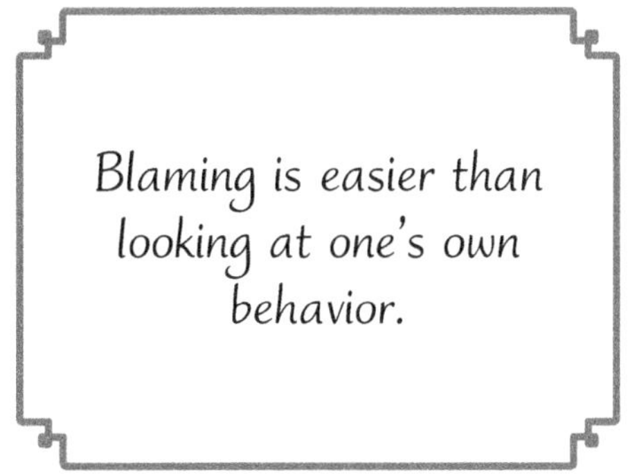

Our ideological self-concept can cause us to self-sabotage. Most of us will do almost anything to protect our perception of who we are, including blaming others or ourselves, using hostility, and sacrificing integrity. We do not see the forest because we are looking at a tree, and it begins in childhood. JonBonét Ramsey's walk portrayed her confidence as a winner. Dependent upon circumstances as an adult, had she lived, her life could have been enriched or hindered by that self-concept.

All of us experience personal difficulties, stressful external factors and learning curves. When up against a challenging situation, successful performers tend to dig in, try harder or seek external motivation. They are accustomed to rallying for challenges. Still, bumping into a Performance Set-Point means that ordinary performance is more difficult to sustain, and paramount performance can become almost impossible. The conscious, creative, dynamic self can actually become immobilized dependent upon the CRS. In other words, given the nutritional value of many foods these days (Set-Point equivalent), Popeye might discover that eating 25 cans of spinach, instead of one, is an insurmountable task.

Extensive fear, guilt, blame and/or shame are excellent indicators for determining when you are against a Set-Point. An honest look at these defensive emotional responses may reveal a pattern which could uncover an underlying CRS imprint. Defining how these emotions relate to your current situation can become the first step in a shift of perception. Without awareness of these emotions and what they mean, you may actually move away from, rather than toward, a goal.

Kermit the Frog, as a tadpole, had 2,353 brothers and sisters. He wondered what the world beyond the swamp had to offer. Others warned him that venturing into the human world was courting disaster. However, he had no time for negative emotions such as fear or guilt. At age 12 he was the first sibling to leave the swamp and one of the first frogs to speak to humans. By leaving his tranquil existence, Kermit looked fear in the face, overcame the odds, discovered the excitement of the movies, the power of a wishing star and was given a "rich and famous" contract by Wideworld Pictures.

Fundamentals

We usually experience fear, blame, guilt or shame when a Set-Point is in conflict with our conscious desires or ideological self-concept.

Charles, a self-employed plumber, loved people. Growing up, there was no extra cash. He felt fortunate to have learned the plumbing trade and liked his work.

As Charles became increasingly successful, there was an unexpected problem. His income was not consistent. He thought his income should be increasing. With assistance, Charles saw the problem. He was a "good guy" who believed in sharing and giving. He perceived that he must help those in need. When a customer was in an obvious jam, when the church toilet needed repair, when a senior citizen or physically challenged person needed help, when anyone tugged at his heart, Charles lent a helping hand at a reduced fee. If he said no, he felt guilty. He had learned it is more blessed to give than to receive. Fear that he was not "good enough" occasionally crept into his thoughts. His Driving Beliefs and ideological self-concept were in direct conflict with his conscious financial goals.

Charles changed his perceptions. He still gave, but more rationally and without sacrifice. He set a prescribed number of hours for charitable work. He learned to say no. He stopped listening to those who would con him. He understood that when some little old lady said she was on an annual fixed income, the fixed amount might be $200,000. He stopped fixing wallets and started repairing toilets.

19

Who You Think You Are Can Keep You Gridlocked

When you recognize persistent resistance to particular behaviors, you may have a perceived role that is in opposition to what you are actually doing. In some people, subconsciously perceived roles are distinctly different than their consciously chosen role, and this issues a golden invitation for a performance struggle. A man wants to be a race-car driver but has been groomed for the priesthood by his family. As a priest his work is admirable but something tugs at him from deep within, and he has a vague resistance to total engagement as a man of the cloth. A young woman longs to be an actress, but her family insists that she learn secretarial skills, a "useful" and financially secure occupation. She may always long for what might have been. A CRS-driven role can cause someone who dreamed of being a film director to end up as a diaper delivery truck driver or federal employee.

A person can be outstanding in early career achievement, even obtain advancement based on performance excellence. Still, role perception somewhere along their path can generate angst and resistance to present career demands. Subtle annoyances can throw them off track. Vague or intense self-restraint can distract their focus. Their performance plateau may vary from restlessness to full out rebellion. Brilliance may be overridden.

In spite of his expertise and favorable standing with management, Calvin became increasingly restless. He felt tired, and at times, wanted to quit. Yet, he did not permit substandard performance.

> Stepping into a dream can also be realized through a twist of fate.

As a child Calvin learned that silence frequently gave him the upper hand. Some of his most stimulating and satisfying experiences were those times when he, in isolation, conquered a challenging project. While pushing toward his dream, Calvin's CRS kept demanding that he keep a low profile. Promotions placed him more and more into the limelight. He became resistant to the very performance he thought would take him to his desired position.

Eventually, Calvin recognized the bidirectional tug on his energies. He came clean with his CEO. Because of his loyalty and valued contributions, he was given more independence, a less prominent office and more personal space. When his subconsciously perceived needs were honored, Calvin's performance again skyrocketed. This man chose to adjust his environment to accommodate his CRS rather than change his imprints to adapt to his goals. Either way, congruency between his subconsciously perceived role and conscious career choices create the necessary balance for peak performance. Achievement at any cost is as unnecessary as a parking lot attendant on a space shuttle.

Stepping into a dream can also be realized through a twist of fate. Lori McKenna, a housewife, began writing songs as a teenager. She dreamed of being a singer-songwriter, but she married her high school sweetheart and birthed five children. She feared her dream was gone; nevertheless, she kept writing songs. At age 36, a twist of fate hit Lori's life in the form of Faith Hill. Ms. Hill recorded three of Lori's songs and they appeared, singing together, on national television.

Lori said, "I wrote to remind myself to keep going and believing."[21] Note that Lori kept *believing* in her dream. Creative time was squeezed in among washing dishes and changing diapers. Her dream required that she write songs. Giving up would have created conflict. By remaining congruent, her dream was realized. Being a housewife and mother was her day-to-day reality, but Lori never sacrificed her dream for the role of mother and housewife.

Lori could have blamed her marriage, become angry at her children or wailed into her mop bucket. She did not. Rather than let daily activities of her career (housewife and mother) cloud out her passion, Lori created space to keep it alive. I ask, was it fate that brought Lori into a fairytale dream come true? Or was it because of her focus, effort and complete alignment?

Michael Ray, in *The Highest Goal*, says "This is the key to grabbing on to your highest goal: You have your own way—your own inner power, your own contribution, your own methods and approaches, and your own experience of the highest goal."[22] It's yours, alone. Most of us have aspirations of going beyond parental influence and CRS imprints. This is an integral component of the teenager's attempt to switch from external to internal values. Sometimes the struggle to separate ourselves from perceived parental tyranny goes unresolved. Thus, we continue to resist, not understanding that, as adults, we are resisting ourselves. The CRS then can pull at us like the undertow of an ocean. Unless we become proactive, we function as if we have never come out of a parental quarantine. Realization of dreams under these circumstances may have greater odds by purchasing a lottery ticket on a boat that is sailing into the Bermuda Triangle.

Fundamentals

Activities that are in opposition to the existing subconsciously perceived personal role will be experienced by the CRS as counter productive.

The national hit television show "American Idol" attracted my attention one night. It was early in the season, and I saw a large number of young people who consciously perceived themselves to be outstanding vocalists. To say that singing talent never graced most of them is a gross understatement. I observed their responses as they came face-to-face with the real-world logic of "You don't have what it takes." I watched as many of them defended their right to be heard again, to be given another try, or to be given a break. They were *certain* they had what it takes to be an American Idol. Sadly, this self-concept was totally incongruous with who they were as vocalists or entertainers.

In their thinking, the judges had made an extreme error. Their perception of their skills and their actual singing abilities were planets apart. In their conscious thinking, their voices are outstanding and they are potential singing superstars.

Yeah, and Donald Duck might become an overnight Metropolitan Opera sensation.

20 Take The Garbage Out: Make Yourself Happy

HAVING READ THIS FAR, YOU KNOW THAT THE subconscious consistently gives the same ol' reactions to the same ol' situations. You know that through the years you can add validating data to the Cellular Response System imprints which maintains cyclic behavior. There is no going-out-of-business sale. If anger is the imprint, a person can instantly become the Priestess of Volcanic Eruptions. If blame is present, even the Blarney stone must lie low. Fortunately, unlike baseball, three strikes does not mean you are out.

Henry was nicknamed Clumsy-Klutz. When he accidentally broke a valuable heirloom at age seven, the family never let him forget it. As Henry grew older, he took on a clumsy-klutz demeanor. At age 17, he was smitten by love. Eventually, he got a date with Karen. For Henry, the night was a disaster. The torment began when he accidentally broke a pottery umbrella stand. Instead of "outgrowing" his clumsiness, it seemed to worsen as more "accidents" occurred. In the office, he gained the reputation of being "Blunder-Man" and became the fall guy for numerous jokes.

In this example, there was repetitious input of reinforcing data to verify that Henry was a clumsy-klutz. He took on the role that others assigned, as well as embellished his own self-fulfilling prophecy. When this happens, imprints are reinforced exponentially. If only Henry could reprogram himself to be a James Bond, he could victoriously tackle his assignment and *always* get the beautiful, sexy woman while at the same time smashing everything in sight.

Too often, like Henry, we hang on to our wounds in some subtle way. Because of our stories, we tend to see ourselves as victimized, or we buy into an assigned label. I do not speak of people who have been mugged, sexually abused, lost their homes to fire, or the like. They often do become devout victims, hindering any possibility of movement in life. For most, self-sabotage emerges via Auto-Reactions and Set-Points. These are the "black sheep," the braggarts, the perfectionists, the jack-of-all-trades people who are so intensely programmed that they have difficulty going beyond their labeled identity. They are also the common achievers who cannot get past their blame, guilt or lack of integrity. They are people who win or inherit millions of dollars and in a few years are as financially strapped as they were before the windfall. They are the perfectionistic people who have a project near perfect, then add "just one more tweak" and the entire thing falls apart.

The great news is that our cell receptors are dynamic. How exciting! Each of us has the ability to alter and direct our lives onto whatever path we choose. The process is simple. *Letting go of an emotionally charged event while engaging the kinesthetic senses renders the event to ordinary information*. Presto! Magically, your AR to those circumstances has been changed. Julia Roberts in the movie *Pretty Woman* took on a new persona when she gained new CRS information. Everyone has this option.

A worthy reminder: when an issue is resolved, only the emotional charge is lost. The memory of the event remains intact and may be retrieved at will. Deciding to live from choice does not mean you must wipe out your memories, prostitute valued beliefs, reenact your past nightmares or varnish your truth. You do not have to become a CRS demolitions expert. You are not practicing voodoo, nor are you on a scientific hunt for etiological pathology. There is no need to analyze your mother's relationship with you. When the President needs different strategies to carry out his agenda, he replaces a cabinet member. Donald Trump had to "reeducate" his hair. He did not grow up with his current hairstyle.

Psychiatrist, Mark Epstein states, "When awareness is hijacked early in life by the need to react to or manage environmental insufficiencies, this hijacking leaves holes in a person's sense of self."[23] Henry fervently wanted to fill that hole by eliminating his clumsiness. With coaching and practice, he actually became quite polished in his ability to meet new people and to move about with ease, thus saving innumerable goblets, heirlooms, knickknacks and other finery. He did all this without watching a single Martha Stewart show.

Periodically, an individual may want to maintain an imprint because it serves them in a positive way. By all means, hang on to those Auto-Reactions that serve you. Randy has an AR that pops up whenever he attempts to cut corners in the middle of a project. He then automatically slows down and increases his focus. This programmed response reminds him that although there is currently no punishing father standing by, he is committed to excellence. A slight reprogramming from "perfection demanded" to "excellence desired" made a tremendous difference in both his attitude and his performance.

You need only deal with those ARs you do not want. Since the memory of programmed events is not eliminated when we let go of their emotional hooks, you may actually use the memory as a reminder or a catalyst. There is no universal law which dictates how you set your values. Nor is there an AR swat team patrolling when, how and whether you create change.

Fundamentals

Set-Points can be changed with new input to the CRS.

Bernice watched the comedy in which her sister, Fay, was playing a key role. The audience laughed openly and often. The cast was immersed in the joy of the play. Bernice had chosen to enter the corporate world. Tonight, as she watched her sister doing what she loved, Bernice realized she had no time for herself, for play, for socializing outside work, no time for love. She felt alone because she *was* alone.

When examining her CRS imprints, Bernice realized how she had been carefully coached by her father. He had insisted that, as a black woman, she must work twice as hard; she must uphold the honor of her race by being a good example; she must "make it." Now, as a successful VP with distinct recognition as a brilliant, hardworking, results-oriented professional, Bernice had done exactly what she was programmed to do.

Fortunately, Bernice did not have to resign in order to change. She identified and eliminated various ARs. She found a new comfort level without sacrificing her integrity or heritage. This woman in her 40s is enjoying dating for the first time since her college days.

Bernice did not change into Winnie-the-Pooh. Eager Beavers rarely turn into Freddie the Freeloader or a Ralph Kramden when CRS programs are altered. The Wicked Witch of the West will not descend upon them with vengeance. They will not sink like a rock in a pond. What they *can* expect is enhanced performance through conscious choice.

21 Your Environment Hoodwinked You: It's Time to Even the Odds

As you navigate through traffic, someone suddenly weaves into your lane, forcing you to slam the brake. Calmly, slowly, you shake your head and say, "I don't know what he's thinking. All the lanes are blocked." Heretofore, you might have yelled at the other driver, called him/her a jerk, shaken your fist, and perhaps divulged the length of your middle finger. This radical change in behavior is the kind of result that defines a shift in the Cellular Response System.

Dr. Bruce Lipton in his course, *Fractal Biology—The Science of Innate Intelligence* reminds us that the cell membrane is homologous to a single-chip microcomputer. It has *literal* capability for programming. Rewiring the CRS occurs because those specific receptors are relieved of the energy charge (usually emotions) that drives their output. They no longer respond reflexively to circumstantial data. Unlike reasoning, will-power, motivational self-talk and positive thinking, no action is required beyond the removal of the charge. Once you defuse the ridiculing attack by your second-grade teacher on your lengthy show and tell, you no longer take offence when someone at the office teases you about your lengthy reports. Of course, if you've earned the ridicule by the kind of reports you submit, you may have to change the reports in order to eliminate the ridicule. Either way, your response will be different. If the rules of the Miss America Pageant change, you can bet that the contestants will change as well. The CRS is no different.

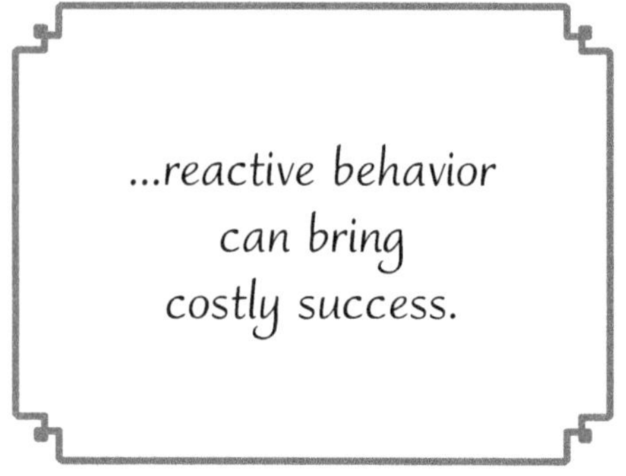

The majority of our limits and struggles are because we so inconsistently behave through conscious choice. Orien, a district attorney, was driven to convict drunk drivers. It was as if the perpetrator became the enemy who had personally wronged him. No one escaped his vindictive push.

The problem Orien eventually faced was that the increased workload began to consume him. Connection with his family waned. Making certain "those drunks" were punished took more and more of his energy. The intense anger that drove his prosecutions was, in actuality, an Auto-Reaction of misdirected rage. Much of his time as a young boy was seized by an alcoholic father who abused both him and his mother. The tie-in to current behavior was almost too obvious.

It is reasonable to assume that Orien would never, in a lifetime, see enough drunk drivers convicted to eradicate the rage he felt for his father. He may as well have spent every afternoon throwing darts at his father's tombstone. In fact, he possibly would have fared better since he then would have actually directed his rage toward the true perpetrator. At the same time he could have built arm muscle and assuaged his internal battle through sheer fatigue.

In Orien's case, as is true in all cellular shifts, the cell receptors held a different code following reprogramming. What previously "pushed his buttons" as a prosecutor no longer carries a charge. Orien is free to respond to instead of reacting to drunk drivers.

I am not saying drunk drivers should not be brought to justice. As Oprah would say, "Don't ya'll write me now! I didn't say that."

Orien is a classic example of how reactive behavior can bring costly success. This scenario is the leader of "success at any price." Spiraling, out-of-control behavior, driven by beliefs and reactive emotions, stands between these individuals and rational thinking. High achievers, this is the difference between success consuming you and being driven to success because you love what you do.

Some of the most insidious ARs start out appearing as favorable or supportive and then become limiting or devitalizing. I know a man who is driven to make certain everyone likes him. At first, this served him well. Management and peers enjoyed his camaraderie. However, it became obvious after awhile that he was spending more time "courting" customers than working. Because he did not curtail this behavior, he lost his job. It is not always the seemingly harmless ARs that nail you. The difficulty lies in the ones you are unaware of, or those that start out great and turn unruly or become antagonistic to your best interest. An analogy might be looking at people you befriend. It's not the jerks that get you, because you know to stay away from them. It's the nice people who have reeled you in and then, for some reason, go sour or turn on you.

Considerable numbers of people are wired to believe that if work is not hard, you are probably playing. Work for them is drudgery, not fun. Finances can also get tied in. If you work and it's fun *and* you get paid, whoa!! That is not permitted, so you slave away at a job you do not like and believe that is the proper thing to do. These people will create hard work regardless of their level of achievement. At risk for them, is personal disservice to themselves. Continuing attenuating reactive behaviors makes about as much sense as a kazoo tuner on an oil rig.

I am reminded of a quote from Arundhati Roy's *The God of Small Things*: "To Ammu, her twins seemed like a pair of small bewildered frogs engrossed in each other's company, lolloping arm in arm down a highway full of hurtling traffic. Entirely oblivious of what trucks can do to frogs."[24] There is no reason to go lolloping blithely through life oblivious to what negative, nonserving beliefs can do. You do not need to blow up the Grand Coulee Dam. Reprogramming can occur with or without conscious knowledge of the original unresolved event.

Reprogramming has been accomplished when we understand and comprehend that our behavior has shifted from reacting to responding. We then have cognitive freedom. We are able to think more clearly. Boredom, frustration and annoying Auto-Reactions are dramatically reduced. Blame, shame, fear and guilt are markedly diminished.

Of course if, like Beetle Bailey, you fail to see these new attributes as valuable, you have the option of continuing just as you are. That, too, is a choice.

Fundamentals

When the body's cell receptors within the CRS are relieved of an emotionally charged experience, those receptors modify and change their response to environmental input data.

Scott felt put down by Saul, his boss. He kept trying to do the "right thing" or say the "right words." The harder he tried, the more difficult Saul became. If Scott met the deadline, the work was seen as sloppy. If he took time to be stringent, he was not fast enough. Scott's approach was to listen more intently, prepare his work with the utmost care, keep his mouth shut and try harder.

Finally, the tension escalated to the point of anger, "You did," "I didn't," "Yes, you did," "I did not." At this point Scott took some time off. He then saw their reactive patterns. Saul was never wrong. Scott's programming demanded that he "get it right." The two of them were a match made in hell, so to speak. Saul never took responsibility for his errors; therefore, Scott was *never* able to "get it right." Saul had no patience for Scott's inability to do exactly what he said to do, whether it was logical or not. Scott kept trying to figure out how to do the right thing.

Eventually Scott left. The movement came after he understood that "getting it right" was an AR that would never be satisfied in Saul's presence. Even though it was difficult to shift, he became stronger and more effective in a number of areas.

I wonder if the Scott-Saul scenario could be the mainspring for a TV reality show? We could stage it at the U. S. capital, add a psychic reader, a javelin toss referee, and have a medical helicopter on standby.

22 Fighting Yourself Is Such a Waste: Battles Suck Energy

HAVE YOU EVER BEEN ENERGIZED FOLLOWING AN ANGRY outburst? Were you ever functioning at a higher level in the presence of fear? (Excluding life-threatening situations.) Chances are high that you were deflated and fatigued following the angry outburst, and somewhat immobilized by your fear. Ordinarily when bumps appear on our path, we deal with them and move on. In the presence of a reactive belief, we frequently end up spinning our wheels in a way that expends a lot of energy. It may feel good to vent, "tell 'em off," recreate the Battle of Gettysburg, or be caught in contemplation about how to get the upper hand. Feeling good notwithstanding, less energy is consumed when we straightforwardly and calmly respond with clarity and purpose. Fairy godmother or circus clown: it is your choice.

The realization that the Cellular Response System utilizes a tremendous amount of energy comes as a surprise to many. Think about it. Somewhere, somehow, deep within your physical body, every nuance of every belief, every memory, every feeling, every tear, every laugh, every reaction and every response is stored as potential. This means that energy is required to hold on to, harness, and on command, emit this information in a split instant. Most know that the entire body operates on electrical energy, the heartbeat is thus driven. Muscles use an electron charge as a functional base for movement. The brain emits waves of energy. Our body-mind is constantly sparking and unitizing energy. Consider anger. The very terms used to describe this passion reflect the immense amount of energy required to express it. He *exploded* in anger. She was *volatile*. The rage overtook him. They were *wild* with anger. She was practically *foaming* at the mouth. We also routinely say such things as "jumping for joy" or "swelling with pride" and "crushed with grief." It is obvious that emotional issues and beliefs require energy both to restrain and to express them.

Our body-mind is constantly sparking and unitizing energy.

Extraordinary amounts of energy sit in the CRS, particularly for its protective and expressive modes. This energy is equal to and sometimes greater than the surge of energy that is used for physical protection. Although it has been labeled as potential energy, it is light years away from being stagnant. Your favorite grandparent, a photograph on the newscast, the wind in a tree, a person's remark or a coworker's stubbornness can spark emotive, highly charged reactions. It makes no difference where you are—in your car, in bed with your private thoughts, or in the bathroom. It makes no difference what the feeling might be—anger, grief, laughter or vulnerability. Energy surges when the CRS launches an AR. Think about the incredible amount of energy that is required for this "imperceptible-until-seen-or-experienced" regulatory system. Now imagine putting all that energy to work in a way that positively supports your performance and your life.

Bert and Arlene worked together for a couple of years. Bert then became a regional consultant. Later, Arlene was dispatched to the southern office to develop cohesive teams. Months later, Arlene was called in for a conference. The CEO had been advised by Burt that Arlene was disagreeable, aggressive and brusque with the branch office staff. Arlene was confused, alarmed and angry at the report. She had been given positive feedback by the staff and felt strongly that she had done a great job. For days, she replayed the data in her head. Obsessive attention was given to "What did I do? What happened? Am I overlooking something? I *know* I did well," and the like.

A great deal of energy was wasted for both parties. Arlene got caught in trying to validate her worth when she already knew it. Her success was a threat to Bert. After submitting the report of lies, Bert had put effort into avoiding Arlene and covering himself with the CEO. Later, after the air was cleared, Arlene was her old self, full of energy and responsive to challenge. As for Bert, power may be the great aphrodisiac, as proclaimed by Henry Kissinger. However, Ben Franklin told us that when a man is wrapped up in himself, the package is quite small.

Generally, a sense of relief and increased vitality is experienced when a subconscious imprint is altered. The body "knows" it will no longer be required to hang on to that conflict and it now has one less reaction to monitor. That energy may now be used in other, more productive ways. Imagine that you have 110 conflicts housed in the CRS. Although, there are many, many times that number. The CRS must constantly assess, record and store millions of pieces of data for *each* of these 110 conflicts in anticipation of the precise moment when all the data collectively says, "React with indignation and anger *now*!" Or, "See? You failed again. You *cannot* do this."

Again and again the same Auto-Reactions to the same Driving Beliefs burn your energy and waste your time. It is possible that Dagwood Bumstead's AR is, "I'm tired. I've gotta lie down now." He has stayed in the same place at work for 50 years. Unless you want to be like him, I suggest that you eliminate a few Auto-Reactions to gain a refreshing spurt of energy to complement your performance.

Yates was placed with Wendy in a transfer. There was no hierarchical status to be claimed by Wendy. Yet she was controlling and insisted on claiming the "right" to instruct Yates on performance and assignment. He nicknamed this adversarial challenger Cruella DeVil. He became resistant and frustrated to the point of wanting to resign. Cruella made his life miserable. Concurrently, Yates began having headaches. Can you see where this is going?

Yates noticed a pattern. Could it be that his headaches were actually being caused by the conflict with Cruella? He looked back to a time in the fifth grade when he had been the target for tongue-lashings by a very mean, and controlling teacher. By releasing the emotional charge on the memory, his present-day "mean-teacher Cruella" had no further hold on him. His headaches disappeared. How's that for an incredibly clear, true example of what we can do to ourselves? Yates could have become belligerent with Cruella or chosen to go off to become a silverware distributor or a tree surgeon. What he chose to do was incredibly more freeing.

Resolution of a reactive belief may not obviously alter the physical health of every person who changes a CRS imprint. Still, there is always an accompanying effect on the physical body. Anytime a person shifts into greater ease, there is a literal enhancement of almost all bodily functions. This holds true whether or not the enrichment is outwardly apparent. It is impossible to change one thing in a system without affecting the whole system.

Shifts in the physical body frequently are accompanied by new "performance spurts," since newly released energy must be utilized. Still, you must routinely take your cerebral cortex to the mental gym for a workout.

Fundamentals

When a Performance Set-Point is altered, the energy that was utilized by the CRS to "be on alert" and the energy that was being used to fight unwanted responses is redistributed to other areas of need in the body.

Sometimes Neil dreaded going to work. He enjoyed being a graphic artist. Yet, his desk was consistently piled with work. He seemed never to be on top of things although tasks were completed with excellence. Something was amiss.

Neil had developed a love for art at a young age. His father, Edward, had wanted him to take over his accounting business. After all, his business was lucrative and he wanted to give his son a good start in life.

At age 10, Neil brought home an Artistic Abilities Award. At the same time, he was about to flunk math. Edward was angry. He accused Neil of deliberately flunking math just to spite him and said Neil would "never amount to anything." The incident was forgotten, but it had been recorded in Neil's CRS.

Assessment of the situation revealed that *success* was the triggering factor for Neil's work angst. To be ultrasuccessful as an artist meant he was making his father wrong. By removing the AR that drove his reticence to perform well artistically, Neil was able to totally engage in his work. The increased energy gave him momentum, and he actually gained a promotion.

Career Tip: Never trust your father to decide which vocation is best for you.

23

Your Brain Begs For Exploratory Freedom

When our ingenious mind power is unleashed, anything from miracles to magic to powerful expressions of mastery can occur. We are not limited. Obviously, most of the time we would not consciously choose to limit ourselves. It is our perception, mechanically bound in our cells, which restricts our thinking, our behavior, our imagination and our skill. Dr. Lipton noted, "Our physiology and behavior patterns conform to the 'truths' of the central voice, be they constructive or destructive beliefs."[25]

Mark operated from the belief that to be the best, he must fully engage. His parents were delighted when his application was accepted by a brokerage firm. Mark "ate, slept, talked and breathed" stockbrokering. After two years, the long hours, extreme competition, and intensive training classes, along with his persistence in building a client base, keeping abreast of the market, and teaching classes to gain exposure, took their toll. He kept trying to enjoy his career, but it became more and more difficult to fully engage.

The work ethic modeled by his parents had been fine for their careers but it was a killer for a stockbroker at the NYSE. It appeared that Mark was engaged in peak performance, but he was actually spinning his wheels. He eventually encountered conflict and opposition to "selling his soul to the company." Resentment began to tax Mark's physical body and his mental attitude. He was being mercilessly driven by an overpowering family role assignment.

Mark let go of his assigned role and tunnel-vision work habits. Now, instead of expending energy in guilt, discontent and nit-picking, he had energy for planning, focusing and creative self-expression. He now made a larger salary and had more time for outside activities. By reacting less he was responding more. As an aside, Mark also found companionship external to the NYSE. Who wants a life without a lover to fight with, or mud to stomp in when things go wrong?

When our stories are "set free," we can be amazingly dynamic. Unrestrained performance is possible because *the absence of the Performance Set-Point permits the creative, logical brain to explore whatever is put before it*. The majority of our faux pas, blunders and constrained behavior can be traced to Driving Beliefs that restrict who we think we are or what we believe we can do. With Auto-Reactions out of the way, a disaster in the making can become a force to be reckoned with.

Your brain-mind is the genesis of intuitive information. The more freedom from ARs and Set-Points you have, the more energy your subconscious can put into collecting data. The more data it collects, the more powerfully it will give back. The more it gives back in the form of hunches, "ahas," and fresh thoughts, the more dynamic your performance can be.

Another amazing thing happened to Mark. Within weeks, his coworkers and associates began to compliment him on the way he handled a client, how he put together a package, and his creative approaches. Mark's brain-mind was functioning as it was designed to. Hunches, understanding and insights came easily. By reacting less, he was responding more. He is not yet the poster child of the NYSE, but anything is possible! With a new outlook on life, more money, a new wife and free time, he could soon require an autographing party for promoting his new book, *Idealism, Perfectionism and Set-Point Nullification*. I must be certain to get a noncompete clause from him.

We would, perhaps, have little identity without beliefs. The problem is that a part of our identity literally *becomes* that person who is associated with the emotions of unresolved events. Driving Beliefs actually individualize and characterize who we are, both to ourselves and to others. As a result, when "buttons are pushed," we tend to define conditions or situations as real, based on a false identity.

Some commonly "assigned identities" associated with less-than-peak performance are: too angry to work with, is interested only in themselves, too fragile, brilliant but lazy, not willing to take a risk, takes too many risks, a loner—doesn't fit in, controlling, a wimp, and others you may well know. Each of these "assigned identities" carries beliefs and perceptions which motivate and actually demand supporting behavior. This is one reason we say such things as, "It's all in his head," or "I can't get it through my thick skull not to behave that way." When we do not understand our own Auto-Reactions, we do not understand others and thus remain in our separation. Unlike Barbie and Ken, we had an earlier life which set our perceptions. Like Clark Kent, we must slip into a different character. Our identity and stimulus-response behaviors require the Supercape of Resolution for transformation of hardwired reactions.

I cannot overemphasize that a shift in CRS hardwiring does not require reliving the past, wallowing in old hurts or digging up traumatic experiences. It is not required that you subscribe to the "no-pain, no-gain" theory of change. Some people wish to know how and why certain beliefs came to be. Others care about that information about as much as a mother wants to dig ditches immediately after her baby is delivered. Removing imprints, not reliving history is the important thing.

Fundamentals

When the Auto-Reactions that make up the Performance Set-Point are eliminated by reprogramming, the Set-Point itself is altered or eliminated.

Early in his life, Ben was placed into a slow reader group. He was upset. His friends were not there. He felt he had been cast away. At times, he would cry during lessons or in the morning when he had to leave for school. As time passed, Ben "bought" the belief that he was a poor reader. Throughout high school and college, he read poorly. He knew the words. No dyslexia was present. There was no dullness of intellect. Ben was quick to learn, but slow reading plagued him.

Reading was not valued in Ben's family. Neither parent completed high school. Neither found excitement, contentment or discovery through reading. They explored life in other ways.

Ben joined the air force. There, he was seen as the intelligent man that he is. He was given special assignments and taught how to read. His Driving Belief, "I'm a poor reader" was overridden. He vowed that his now-treasured reading skill would take him far. Upon discharge, he was hired by IBM where he became a high-ranking executive.

Ben's struggle came from the Ghost of Teacher Past. Participating in a wet T-shirt contest does not make anyone a lingerie expert. Standing in front of a classroom full of students does not make a person a teacher. Oops! I have to go now and check out an Auto-Reactive of judgment about certain teachers.

24

Confusion Is Not the Enemy: Hang in There

When the Cellular Response System is in opposition to personal resolve or creative efforts, you may experience what feels like bewilderment or disequilibrium, when, in fact, it is only conflict. This is true whether you are facing a decision, headed for a goal or planning a program. The conflict is real and can be overbearing. Increasing frustration may appear because of efforts to direct the environment or consciously control outcomes. It's like trying to jump ship (goal) and Captain Hook (Auto-Reactions) snags you again and again just as you dive.

Overall, conflict and confusion are decreased with almost all CRS changes. During the actual shift, however, temporary confusion may be present. Any number of things can occur. In the midst of the "switch-over," some people momentarily feel that nothing has happened. Others report a sense of relief. Sometimes the change is immediately apparent and blatant. The shift may be subtle, later appearing as a realization that an automatic behavior is no longer present. An example might be noticing that you no longer feel antagonized by certain behaviors in others. It might now be immaterial that your colleague is a wimp.

Confusion is present in the midst of change, usually before new behavioral parameters have been defined. This holds true under circumstances that bear no relationship to the CRS. When you move into a new home, there is confusion. The home may be lovely, just what you wanted, the location ideal and the family happy to move. Still, there is an initial disruptive feeling. The habit of walking out the bedroom door and turning left must be changed because the stairway in this house is to the right. In the middle of the night, the refrigerator is definitely in the "wrong" place. In time, though, your brain gets the messages and the confusion disappears. It is much the same when shifting the hardwiring of the CRS. New parameters exist. You may feel "spacey" or a bit uncertain during the switch, but that will resolve itself.

Verna was offered a promotion to director of training. It was an optimal job, but Verna had a fear of public speaking. As training director she would be required to teach classes for personnel from a wide area who came to the university for advanced education. The opportunity was huge, but Verna was concerned that fear would cause her to fail.

After some reprogramming, to Verna's amazement, she felt confident. She was given a trial run as speaker for an upcoming program. The hour arrived. As Verna sat in the wings waiting for an introduction, she felt a bit of anxiety. What if that "CRS stuff" didn't "take"? What if her nervousness increased and she was unable to deliver? When her name was called, Verna strolled to the lectern, turned toward the audience and started speaking. Her legs began to shake, but with determination, she delivered her opening remarks.

Later, Verna reported a mixture of subtle fear, anticipation, excitement, confusion and desire. However, about a quarter of the way through her presentation, everything shifted. Verna discovered that she loved being in front of this large audience. She felt absolute clarity. The presentation was a breeze, and she felt her entire body tingle with pleasure. Backstage, she exclaimed, "Yes! Yes! I can do this."

Verna demonstrated another benefit of CRS changes. After the dust settles, there is an increased clarity. The greater awareness a person has of their surroundings and their situation, the greater the chance of survival, growth, development and continuance. Archie Bunker often *thought* he was aware. General Patton *made* himself aware through constant assessment and reassessment of each situation he faced. Of course, we must consider the intellectual abilities of each of these men if we are to compare them. Archie, by Hollywood design, had negative, stereotypic thinking, whereas General Patton was a brilliant and revered general. Still, the metaphor holds true. Clarity enables our intellect to generate magnificent phenomena. When full cognition and a boundless subconscious are working together, there is no need for Santa Claus.

Archie Bunker made us laugh, but he was never a blazing achiever. His beliefs and perceptions kept him in a state of hyperreaction. (Why do I occasionally identify with him?) General Patton had both clarity and congruency. He won his battles and left behind timeless management principles. One of those principles says, "Never fight a battle when nothing is gained by winning."[26] You cannot gain by fighting the CRS because you are fighting yourself. Yes, establishing and living "by design" is possible. We can positively direct our behavioral programming. Jack Kornfield beautifully portrays a congruent CRS in the following excerpt from *A Path With Heart*.

> "Sylvia Boorstein. . . illustrates this power with a story of . . . a famous doctor who for many years had served as president of the American Psychiatric Association. He was known as a gentleman, a man of integrity and kindness, who brought great joy to everything in his life. He always offered a deep respect to his patients and

> colleagues. After he retired and grew older, he started to become senile. He lost his memory and his ability to recognize people. He still lived at home.... Being longtime friends, Sylvia and her husband ... were invited to his home for dinner.... It had been some time since they had last seen him, and they wondered if his senility had increased. They arrived at the door with a bottle of wine and rang the doorbell. He opened the door and looked at them with a kind of blank stare that showed no recognition of who they were even though they had been friends for many years. Then he smiled and said, 'I don't know who you are, but whoever you are, please come in and enjoy my home,' and he offered them the same graciousness with which he had lived for his whole life." [27]

Each of us is responsible for reducing the conflict and frustration in our own lives. Each of us is responsible for deciding who we will be and how we will behave. Each of us is responsible for growing our own impossible dream.

In California, I once had a Mexican waiter who demonstrated congruency, clarity and focus. I asked to take home part of my meal, but left the box on the table. This man ran to me as I walked toward my car. When he handed me the box, I noticed these letters had been written across the top: G.H.L.W.MEX.P.LSB, XLIX. Curiosity grabbed me and I asked what the letters meant. Patiently, he pointed to each letter and explained, "I don't want to forget. It is, 'Gray-Haired Lady With Mexican Pink Long-Sleeve Blouse at Table 49.'" That is intention.

Fundamentals

When reprogramming alters the Performance Set-Point, confusion and conflict are decreased.

Paul knew he should be angry, but he did not feel angry. He felt confused. A coworker had just made the sort of comment that heretofore would have sent his mind into a tailspin or a rampage. Two weeks ago, he was feeling restless, frustrated and bored. At times he thought some members of the team were incompetent. But Paul had changed some imprints. He saw that his boredom was the same as much of his childhood. There had been no intellectual challenge from his teachers. He also saw that he had been operating with the belief that he must work at the same pace as everyone.

After today's comment, he had decided to take some alone time. The confusion was new. As he sat there, something began to "perk" and suddenly he got it. Insensitive comments from his coworkers were no longer capturing his ego! His confusion dissipated.

Over the weekend, Paul devised a plan that allowed him to remain a team member and work at his own pace while others did the same. He was amazed that he had not thought of this before. When the plan was submitted to management, it was adopted for the entire department.

This is a case where Rolaids did not spell relief, and neither extra rounds of golf nor Monday night football would have appeased the boredom.

25

Confidence Can Spiral into Self-Assuredness: You're Amazing!

THESE DAYS THERE IS SIGNIFICANT TALK ABOUT LIVING in the moment, being fully present and creating your reality. Much of that commentary is made in conjunction with spiritual development directives. While many of those recommendations have value, I have zero interest in convincing you that peak performance requires captivating "presence" or adherence to daily ritual. It is more important to understand the value of removing oppositional data from your CRS. Being present is but one advantage. For emphasis, a few are repeated here. Discernment, insight, creativity and the ability to focus will automatically increase. There can be more extensive guidance through intuitive feedback. The autonomic nervous system which controls activities such heart rate and gut motility has greater balance. The immune system and psyche have greater integrity. Cognition is maximized. Unless you want to end up feeling like a cross between James Bond and Tim Allen, this is the way to go.

Being present does not mean that other aspects of your life are ignored or forgotten. The old cliché, "He lived for the moment," is quite different than "living *in* the moment." An addict lives *for* the moment, the rush, the escape, the high. An individual who is living *in* the moment is seen as fully present and capable of readily collecting, giving, receiving and assessing information without the encumbrance of defensive, protective or other interruptive behavior. Whether we can consistently be fully present each moment of our lives is open for discussion. Still, overwhelming evidence shows that eliminating beliefs and perceptions that interfere with choice and performance makes us happier and more content.

One night, I received a phone call from a friend who was at the local hospital emergency room. "I cut off my thumb," he said. In my surprise and horror, a cliché spontaneously flashed from my mouth. "What!?! Where was your head?" That question is often asked when we have difficulty believing what we think is a stupid act. The intent of the question is, "Your mind had to be elsewhere. You could not have been thinking clearly." In other words, "You were not focused on what you were doing." The previous day, my friend had argued with his son, who bitterly opposed his father's recent divorce.

"As I pushed the wood, I was not even aware that my thumb was in front of the blade," he said. This man earns his livelihood by designing and making beautiful, custom, fine furniture. He has pushed thousands of pieces of wood past saw blades. This time, however, he was not present, not focused. Remnants of the argument with his son were still knocking around in my friend's head. Yes, he took an accurate measurement. Yes, he set the saw fence to the correct distance. Yes, he adjusted the blade to the proper height. These operations are automatic for this man. His thumb is gone today, though, because of his lack of awareness.

This graphic example may not seem germane to your situation. I assure you that the concept, the application, is the same whether you are playing racquetball or closing a billion dollar deal. It is mind-boggling how many business deals, hobbies, vacations and the like are defeated or negatively affected due to lack of presence during transactions. Comments such as, "What the ___ was I thinking," "I can't believe I did that," "Can you believe I just blah, blah, blah?" are generally the result of not having been focused when a transaction or behavior occurred. The consequences of the lack of clarity can vary immensely. Certainly, not a lot of divorces cause a man to end up minus a thumb, even though some may *feel* as though they lost an entire hand. Still, we must pay attention.

Overt inattentiveness causes us to ignore valuable intuitive information. How many times have you been given but disregarded a hunch? Ernest said, "*I had a feeling* I should go a different way, but I was in a hurry." His car was totaled when someone did not stop for a red light. Ernest's mind reached far beyond what he could consciously perceive, assessed the situation and "told" him to choose another route. When he gave apprehensive concern priority over intuitive feedback, he placed his life in jeopardy. Intuition is not a barracuda seeking to be fed, nor does it wish to be ignored. The intuitive mind serves us 24/7, but we must listen closely. Rarely does it ask for an audience with "Your Majesty."

Frequently, behaviors are blamed on stress, almost as if that gives us the right to lash out in anger or stubbornly refuse to cooperate. Most so-called stress lies in our interpretation of our environment. An example is the way in which some divorced couples end up as friends while others are constantly embroiled in bitter personal or court battles. Ellen was divorced 38 years ago. She continues to be bitter, and repeatedly attempts to "get even" with her ex-husband. Again and again, she bad-mouths him to their children, and believes that he still owes her. She is "stressed out." How could a man have even a trace of desire to stay with such a negative, faultfinding, punitive woman? Bozo the Clown would have difficulty continuing to make merry.

Stress is not the culprit. Walt Kelly summed this up through Pogo: "We have met the enemy and he is us."[28] Most of us tend to accept consciously collected information and observed signs as absolutes. Our perception taints our reception and assessment of data and, thus, affects our choices. The filter (perception) that a brash, agitated genius sees through is vastly different than the filter of an equally intelligent, quieter, focused person. We cannot cite stress as the cause of *or* lack of performance.

In summary, I reiterate that creativity in thinking, planning, implementation and performing can become the norm. Trust is heightened when you consciously direct your life. You are less prone to prejudge others, which means you can listen more effectively. As you are more accepting of others, they tend to return the same behavior. Confidence continues to build as challenges are successfully met with competence. When confidence is built on top of confidence, a spiraling level of self-assuredness, self-reliance and composure emerges.

For years, I was a consultant to VA hospitals. Once, the staff introduced Tom, a patient whose overbearing attitude and incessant desire for coffee was creating havoc on the ward. He literally took cups of coffee from the hands of others, stole it off the food cart, bribed, lied and did almost anything to get coffee. A staff member told me, "He even traded his dentures for a pot of coffee." My immediate response was, "I don't need to see this man. I want to see the man who took his dentures. He's the one who has a *real* problem!" You can get an inkling of just how far the human spirit can travel down the path of self-destruction. Granted, these men were confined to a psychiatric unit. Surely, though, at one time, they had dreams and goals just as we all do. The point is, anything can be carried to extremes, including focus. The important thing to glean from this story is that we need to foster new understanding of ourselves so that out of these understandings, new ideas, new ways of structuring our lives and new levels of performance can emerge. Forrest Gump had that clarity. Look at all he accomplished! Les Brown, a motivational speaker, says that each of us has greatness within. Each of us has a responsibility to find it and live it.

Fundamentals

Personal fulfillment and the physical body are enhanced because of living in the present moment.

Frances was a general practitioner who also held a doctorate in philosophy. She and her patients enjoyed each other. Her initial career was teaching philosophy at the state university. Weary and dissatisfied, she went to medical school. A few years into practice found Frances again weary and restless.

It was easy to understand her reactive behavior. Frances wanted to be a farmer, but her parents convinced her that a woman could not earn a living as a farmer. They feared she would become exasperated with the enormity of farming, or that her keen intellect would not be stimulated. Her CRS imprint was, "You must use your intellect wisely. You're too smart for ordinary work. You're a woman. Women can't successfully run farms."

By changing her Set-Point, Frances relieved the angst. Instead of giving up her practice, she began to study organic farming and purchased acreage in the countryside. She now commutes to her part-time practice. Frances and her husband are gradually building an organic farming business. She can leave her practice or stay. Meanwhile, feet and hands are in and on the soil. Instead of longing for what might have been, Frances now feels the joy of doing what she loves.

You can take the country girl to school, but you can't take the country out of the schoolgirl. I wonder: Should Frances's patients still bring her fresh tomatoes and corn, or should she bring her produce to them?

Part 2

"We are what we repeatedly do.
Excellence, then, is not an act but a habit"

—Aristotle

Your Family Told You Who to Be: Is That Still Okay With You?

Specific roles are assigned to us by Significant Others. Generally, the family is responsible for these basic role assignments, but they may come from anyone in a prominent, paramount position. Roles are accepted, usually because of repetitive, prevailing directives from those who, early on, mold our lives. As we develop, the regulatory components of their beliefs about who we are or should be defines character and responsibility. These personifications get transposed into Driving Beliefs which then compel us to maintain the assigned role. Some individuals take on opposing roles by their refusal to do what the family demands. Others take a particular role as they rebel against family dogma. In a convoluted way, these roles are still assigned since it is because of the family that the role has been taken. Regardless of how a role has been implanted and accepted, the accompanying Driving Beliefs dominate personal behavior. Whenever there is an internal clash or external discord, role observance usually takes precedence.

A child placed in the role of "Helper" may decide to become a minister. If s/he consciously wishes to connect with others, make a difference in the world, or has other compatible goals, the mandated role could then enhance performance. Unless other goals are actualized to the point of precipitating conflict with the accepted role, all goes well. If, on the other hand, the individual sees greener pastures or grows weary of being the "Helper," s/he may become unhappy, disillusioned, "burned-out" or depressed. This is considered a role crisis. There has been a collision between the accepted driving role and personal desire. This individual may have grown weary with their assigned role. Personal growth could have uncovered preferred roles or given insight into how they were designated as the "Helper." Rebellion against the role might occur, or the role of "Helper" may have been combined with a secondary-choice role of "helping to heal the planet" which also fit with the assigned role. Later, different, more exciting opportunities appeared, causing the "Helper" role to be diminished in priority. The potential complexities are endless.

Other beliefs, such as, "I must obey," or reinforcements like parental rewards or acts of nature, such as death, come into play. In a role conflict, life is going great, the career is developing nicely, the chosen job has materialized, and suddenly you hit a wall or come up against a block. All sorts of feelings can emerge at this time. One individual may find themselves in a situation that seems to have been a theme in their life. Others experience the feeling that "one more time they have been used by the system." Some get passed over for a desired assignment or experience circumstantial setbacks. A driving role can cause people to sabotage their own efforts or keep them from attaining a dream. In yet other role assignments, an individual seems almost prohibited from going where they want to go careerwise. Think of George Bailey in the movie *It's a Wonderful Life*.

I am not speaking of life career assignments given by SOs. A journalist, for example, may have been consistently expected to follow in the footsteps of a parent. Here, the career is not necessarily role-assignment related. This person could have had the role assignment of the Brilliant One or the Responsible One. They then could combine the assigned role of the brillant one with the career of journalist. If s/he does poorly as a journalist, there will be conflict.

Actualizing an entirely new role will be difficult, if not impossible, until an assigned role is set free. You may have observed individuals struggling to change their role, profession or career. The desired role is rumbling around internally, like a silent scream wanting to be heard. Many do make the switch, but almost always, it is done after a Performance Plateau or a Role Crisis. More and more, we are seeing dramatic changes in career choices as people reach a different level of maturity during midlife. Some of these changes are admissible, in part, because of increased longevity of life. Still, they must find a way—sometimes through rationalization related to their stage of life—to set aside their assigned role.

Some common roles and how they, through the CRS, affect success are given here. Many high achievers have some of the traits in all these roles because of associated characteristics. I invite you to analyze your current situation. Observe and identify your own Driving Beliefs associated with your personal performance roles. You may possibly see how they have been transplanted to behavior and reactions in current situations. Naturally, there is space here for discussing only a few roles. You, yourself, can best define your own assigned role. There are as many roles as there are individualistic families to define and create them. However, the following examples offer a model for analysis of role behavior, whether they be different or similar. Some may seem extreme. All are real.

Be aware that there is overlapping of the roles we take on or give to ourselves. A Black Sheep may take on a subrole of Savior in an attempt to counter the family's assigned role. The Helper may secondarily be The Perfect One, and so forth. Yours may be entirely different than those mentioned. Generally, however, each of us has a predominant role which drives us. A valuable asset to going *Beyond Best* is to identify and foster any desired changes in your prevailing role.

The Renegade Role

The Renegade, by definition, rejects conventional rules and decorum. They make their own laws and can become defiant. This is especially true when the Renegade's motive or behavior is questioned, or when they are requested to follow customary or prevailing circumstances that conflict with their own ideas or actions. Underlying their behavior is an imprint that says, "Nobody tells me what to do." A fascinating trait is that this individual may literally walk away from something they really enjoy or desire because the drive to defy is so deeply or broadly embedded within the CRS.

Somewhere along the way, through wounding or for survival purposes, the Renegade adopted the Driving Belief that resistance, brazenness, impudence and noncompliance were the best, if not the only, ways to win at life. Their CRS is in constant surveillance mode for opportunities to resist, confront, outdare, challenge or dispute conventional reasoning or overt commands. Through Auto-Reactions, their common sense or wisdom may be cast aside, even if their conscious mind does not agree. Interestingly, the Renegade may actually have a conscious awareness that they are "cutting off their nose to spite their face," and proceed with rebellious behavior anyway.

When encountering a Performance Plateau, the Renegade may experience any or all of the common responses associated with any Performance Plateau: guilt, blame, shame and fear. However, the Renegade has a tendency to put greatest focus on blame. Their underlying fear is very real but buried deeply under insolence. As the struggle crescendos because the plateau is more and more unconquerable, this person may self-destruct. There is usually an inability to overcome the immense fear that no one really understands or cares about them. The Renegade rarely will stand in that fear or let others know it exists. The fact that they can never totally trust anyone causes them, through Auto-Reactions of lashing out and running away, to collapse the few benevolent connections they do have.

Essence:

The Renegade may long to be at peace or to be understood.

The Black Sheep Role

The Black Sheep is the discreditable member of the family or, in later life, the business. Usually this is because they disregard codes of conduct or tell the truth, disclosing family—or business—secrets. These individuals do not fit in because their thinking and behavior are overtly different. They may be an embarrassment to the family who judges their "dirty deeds" or reckless behavior as betrayal, shameful or disreputable. Whether they are shunned because of different behavior, or have been chosen to be the Black Sheep, they are the outsider. They are seen as childish and selfish, and may be targeted for criticism, sarcasm and hostility. Since the Black Sheep is identified as bad, or the teller of family secrets, they frequently are seen as the one who causes all the problems. Yet, surprisingly, they can be the one who holds the family together.

The Black Sheep may be an overachiever or have lack of worldly success. This outcome is based on how, early on, they learned to cope with their outcast position. Either way, when faced with a Performance Plateau, the Black Sheep may appear confident of their stance and uncaring about the situation. They may outwardly blame others for their lack of continued success. However, underneath their outward presentation, they have beliefs such as, "I don't really belong. I don't fit in. My goals are too different. I don't know how to play their game. I'm not liked as well as the others." These perceptions tend to highlight their internal fear of rejection and increase their guilt and shame when not achieving. The CRS will give Auto-Reactions that support their rejection or lack of success. Achievement can give them the illusion that all is well and "prove" that they are as "good" as anyone.

The family may also label a member as a Black Sheep because they choose something other than that which the family ordains. For example, a family who has for generations been staunch Republicans may shun a member who becomes a candidate for a Democratic office. This individual has chosen to be an outsider and the family separates them out.

The Black Sheep overtly states, "I couldn't care less about what others think of me." The truth is, they isolate themselves because of the tension created by their behavior. At the same time, they consciously think, "I might as well do what I want to because they already think I'm crazy." This behavior further sets them apart and subsequently emphasizes their separation. Guilt and shame for the cyclic behavior reinforces the CRS programming. The resulting increased fear of continued rejection (even of themselves, by themselves) compounds their inability to be a part of the team. They may try harder and do more, but things just do not fall into place. Their Performance Plateau is very real since the team is necessary to reach goals, to be supported for promotions, to gain assistance in development of programs and so forth. The thing the Black Sheep resists the most—being an integral part of the group— is, on a much deeper level, the very thing they fear *not* being.

Essence:

The Black Sheep may long to be the "star," or to belong.

The Brilliant/Competent/ Successful One Role

The Brilliant/Competent/Successful One has been programmed to believe that their intellectual prowess and abilities exceed those of others. They, therefore, have a covenant to responsibly use their talents. Frequently, these people are given missions or accountability beyond customary norms, along with relentless or pushy dictates, or have been burdened with excessive praise and rewards for success. In either case, the CRS says, "You must consistently use your knowledge to outperform others. You must be successful." If the Brilliant/Competent/Successful One is eccentric or has equally intellectually bright siblings, they may have the responsibility of being supersuccessful added to their role.

I have placed Brilliant, Competent and Successful together for simplicity and will call this role the Brilliant One for the same reason. It is ordinary for an individual to be singularly assigned to any one of these roles. However, there are general characteristics that follow all of them.

For the Brilliant One, genius can be expected even in areas about which they know little or nothing, as well as in their areas of proficiency. The pressure is on to perform with intellectual agility, regardless of the circumstances and irrespective of what is felt or desired. Constant learning is required. These people can never know enough. High levels of accomplishment often means that more and more must be done since they must go beyond expectations of ordinary accomplishment. Blaming or sitting in judgment of others who do not quite "get it," or who perform at levels considered as substandard by the Brilliant One, is common. Think of Major Charles Winchester III in the TV series *M*A*S*H.*

Auto-Reactions will dampen enthusiasm for ordinary or "imperfect" preferred activities, and can prohibit a less demanding schedule. Even hobbies may take on an air of work since the Brilliant One is compelled to be absolutely competent in whatever task is approached. Auto-Reactions can cause self-sabotage when this person is placed in an unfamiliar context because they are acutely aware that they have little to offer. Reaching a Performance Plateau means overwhelming guilt and shame because they cannot successfully move forward. Fear that others are more brilliant, that they will disappoint the team or that they have nothing to offer, can then affect performance. If caught in a lull, they are their own worst critic and depression can overcome them.

There are instances in which an individual's level of brilliance does not match the expectations inherent in the assigned role. In short, they are not as competent as the family has deemed them to be. These individuals are in an even more difficult situation because intensity of effort is compounded by their limitation. In order to save face, this person may attempt to hide out when the going gets rough.

ESSENCE:

May long to be "ordinary."

The Absorber Role

The Absorber has learned to take on whatever happens around them. They suck up, endure and bear the hardships. Their mission is to learn everything they can about a given situation, figure out the lay of the land and take on the resolution. The load can get quite heavy, but they will continue to take on more, especially to assist those around them in getting what they need. The Absorber's CRS says, "I can handle it. Watch me. I can take care of everything. I know what to do to make things *right*." They are always on the alert for whatever action is coming down the pike. The Absorber is dependable and will get things done, although it may be at personal cost.

Fatigue and impasses are not permitted. Their Will appears tenacious. They swing into action quickly and continue until closure is realized. At times, it may appear they do not need the team, but in actuality they use the team quite effectively to feed or drive their own behavior. The Absorber may push team members a bit more than they want to be pushed, but the goal is the completion of the task rather than a personal vendetta. As a result, they sometimes feel alone even in the presence of many. Life can be lonely for the Absorber because they have difficulty with intimacy. At the same time, they can choose to be loners since they must take on the task of soaking up the fallout around them. Auto-Reactions demand that they engage themselves wholly in addition to being the individual who can transform circumstances.

When the Absorber is placed in the position of being an "ordinary team member," Auto-Reactions compel them to maneuver into a more prominent position. They are unhappy unless taking on the impact of a situation or handling the adversities of others. If the team members want or enjoy this, all is well. However, when more than one Absorber, or others such as The Responsible One or the Brilliant One, are also team members, there may be trouble in the camp.

Reaching a Performance Plateau for the Absorber often means they have been placed in a position where they cannot take on the "I can correct this" lead. In other situational plateaus, their Auto-Reactions cause them to take on more and more. Their physical limit can rear its ugly head. The Absorber is then in a dilemma. "How can I keep going?" Yet they must. Some quit, thus taking off the heat for a while until physical stamina returns. They are more likely to make a lateral shift in order to maintain their raison d'etre. A few become ill. Most have difficulty letting others take the lead even though they may request them to do so.

In the extreme, fear that they are not doing what they *should* be doing or not helping another can immobilize them, although not for long. Blame and guilt are prevalent. The Absorber may or may not consciously recognize that they are stuck in a cycle. Taking care of business, knowing what to do and when and how to do it, regardless of their own needs, prevails.

Essence:

May long to be free or to be taken care of.

The Lazy One/ Loser Role

The Lazy One/Loser sometimes puts on a great front or may speak a great line. However, close inspection reveals little follow-through. Promises are a significant part of their repertoire. When requests are made of them, they will promise to fulfill it, perhaps even give a time frame. However, little, if anything, gets accomplished. The actions of the Lazy/Loser scream their intentions in the presence of words that say the opposite. Just as often, the response can be, "No way. I'm not doing that."

Lazy/Losers are quite smart. Their sharp intellect is probably an integral component in the development of their role. Early on, they used this acuity to learn how to manipulate situations to their advantage, often earning praise as they did so. At some point, they were designated the Lazy One or the Loser because SOs were unable to outwit them and gave up trying to change their behavior, were too lenient, permissive or helpful and lost power, or because they never established their role as the authority in times of rebellion. The Lazy/Loser took the upper hand and learned to shirk independent responsibility.

In the work situation, the Lazy/Loser may show competence until there is a task or assignment that he or she dislikes. If they decide they are not going to do something, persuasion and commanding does not budge them. Since they are accustomed to hearing others speak of disappointment and frustration with them, these words fall on deaf ears.

The Lazy/Loser has a CRS that says, "What I need will come to me. No need to strain myself. I don't have to take responsibility for anything unless I want to." A Performance Plateau for this person may be reached when they are backed into a corner because of financial stress, or when they encounter someone who maintains authority and can outwit them. The most intense feeling for the Lazy/Loser who is caught in this situation is fear. They may attempt to blame others, but confrontation about their own behavior generally dissipates accusations; at least, overtly. They may continue to harbor blame and/or become sullen and stubborn. Generally, the Lazy/Loser will quit rather than accept responsibility, even if they are personally negatively affected. Their Auto-Reactions can rather quickly cause them to self-destruct.

Essence:

May long to be the "apple of someone's eye" who cares enough to call their bluff.

The Responsible One Role

The Responsible One performs to the maximum in everything they commit to undertake. When the going gets tough, they get tougher, do more, stand taller. If a goal seems impossible, these people will figure out a way to accomplish what they have set out to do. They keep going when others have stopped. Accountability is paramount. The tendency is for the Responsible One to take on more than their share of assignments and to tackle a larger chunk of the task at hand. At all costs, they must be answerable for their conduct and conscientious in fulfillment of their obligations. Right and wrong can be a significant characteristic of their thinking. At the same time, their concept of right and wrong can be somewhat narrow, i.e. judgment of others comes easily. Expanding the Responsible One's thinking in terms of right and wrong may be difficult to take on since their definitions are narrowly limited. Deep inside they feel inadequate and insecure, so must judge and label others in order to boost themselves.

Achievement appears to be rather cut and dried for the Responsible One but, internally, it comes at great cost. Their CRS is programmed to drive their behavior beyond reason even in simple tasks. "I can do this. I can do it well. I do it better than anyone else." Where others might complete a task and move on, the Responsible One is compelled to go beyond the ordinary and perhaps overdo or overrespond. Because intense Auto-Reactions demand responsibility regardless of conscious predilection, name-calling of others, anger, verbal abuse and hostile behavior may emerge. Paradoxically, this is, in part, because the Responsible One usually is not responsible to themselves, to their own desires and preferred choices. Their integrity may be at stake when it comes to monitoring responsibility for the self. Visible, responsible achievement must come first.

Auto-Reactions drive the Responsible One to the extent that physical illness can occur because of over-responding to their need to be responsible in everything they do. The incongruence between responsibly implementing assignment after assignment and freeing themselves to pursue their own wishes and dreams creates a self-contradictory, inherent helplessness. Excuses may be given when work they have done does not meet their high standard, but they may, themselves, believe that the excuse is invalid. They seldom, if ever, grant themselves redemption.

Performance Plateaus may surface when the Responsible One gets in over their head, is burned out because of the intensity of their involvement, has taken on more activities than can be handled, or continues to disallow personal choice in accepting tasks. The CRS says, "You must, at all costs, do the responsible thing, always." When they run low on energy or lack conscious drive to continue, it becomes easier and easier to blame others when things go wrong or go undone. Guilt keeps the Responsible One from moving into what they view as the selfish behavior of taking care of their own needs first. Their persistent blame can alienate them from others. Their guilt paralyzes efforts to change their stance. Shame that they want something for themselves can be extensive as well. Undergirding the blame, shame and guilt is the pervading fear that to give up being totally responsible means ultimate supreme punishment.

Essence:

May long to be carefree and unencumbered.

The Perfect One/ Good One Role

The Perfect One/Good One has the untenable task of living and working flawlessly. Everything they do must be without defect or blemish. Their rewards, early on, were based on whether they were being good, doing the right thing, "behaving," giving the "right" answers, being orderly, blameless and similar impossible directives. Now they must learn the rules and follow them precisely. Along with perfection there may come an element of dependency which presents itself as possessiveness. In other words, the Perfect/Good One may subconsciously confuse being needed with excellence. Being perfect, doing the best job, even if it means a heavier work load, in their eyes, means that they have increased value.

The possessiveness about their work is resultant of the subconscious connection between being perfect and being revered. The Perfect/Good One attaches themselves to their work in such a way as to create a need for their services. By so doing, they hope to be irreplaceable. At the same time, their Auto-Reactions disallow mediocre performance. If they dare to be careless or naughty, the guilt is extreme because of accompanying fear that they will fall into disfavor. These individuals work diligently to show the team that they are certain and sure, that they can handle the job as well as, and probably better than, anyone else.

Blame is a close companion of the Perfect/Good One because when others are wrong or less than perfect, it may reflect on them. They believe this then makes them look bad or have less favor. If they are stressed and others do less than what the Perfect/Good One deems as perfect, blame is rampant. They have zero tolerance for incompetence. In great part, this is because they tire of having to be perfect themselves. Being consistently perfect or good requires time and a great deal of energy which can be depleting.

Their CRS says, "When you are perfect/good, you are admired and esteemed." Therefore, if mistakes are made or a Performance Plateau is reached, shame is acute and intense. Anyone, including themselves, who is less than perfect, is a loser in their eyes. Of course, their own underlying fear is that of rejection because they lose value when less than perfect. In addition, they are burdened with the fear of failure. This means that taking risks is a tricky business. It makes these people too vulnerable. The possibility of personal exposure is too great. The Perfect/Good One needs to know all the parameters in order to be on top of the situation. Their fear of what negative thing might happen (conscious or not) far outweighs the fact that the unknown could be positive and exciting. Difference is permitted, but only to the extent that they feel confident that they have the ability to maintain their outstanding perfection. Fear and shame related to potential failure can be too overwhelming to permit bold new steps or risk-taking.

Performance plateaus can be a frequent visitor to the Perfect/Good One. Their Auto-Reactions require tremendous amounts of obsessive planning, re-implementing, re-negotiating, reemphasizing, re-researching, and reevaluating to maintain their unobtainable perfection. They are not permitted to make a mistake. If they see roadblocks, they often think it is better to give up than to risk being a failure. Thus, they begin to think, "Why try?" This kind of thinking can immobilize them. Making the ideal real is their nemesis.

Essence:

May long to be loved regardless of whether or not they are perfect.

The Troublemaker Role

THE TROUBLEMAKER IS A PROVOKER WHOSE MODUS OPERANDI is to interrupt the status quo by making others uncomfortable. When they stir up trouble, create agitation in others, cause them to worry or be inconvenienced, the Troublemaker can choose one of two options. They can put the spotlight on themselves and bask in the limelight, or they can hide behind the chaos they have precipitated. Whatever their choice, they are daring to defend themselves and their rights. Then, in the midst of the chaos, they do whatever they choose to do in order to get the job done or to shirk responsibility. They know how to take the heat off themselves and can be quite skilled at making others uncomfortable at the same time. This often gets them what they want. Troublemakers are willing to do whatever it takes to achieve their goals. They can lay specific, elaborate strategies to disrupt a process they believe to be unfair, or in a few moments can create impromptu chaos to undo or promote change. Whatever they do usually causes distress, disturbance or difficulty in the ranks.

Ordinary steps of problem solving may be too cumbersome, too time consuming, have too many roadblocks or seem illogical for the Troublemaker. Their keen sense of justice and high level of creativity coupled with tenacious stick-to-it-iveness skills enables them to tramp in with combat boots where others fear to tread even lightly in velvet slippers. Cause and effect as seen by these individuals may not always be seen as logical by others. The Troublemaker can see that the cause is not necessarily the problem, and therefore, favorably separate the two in order to produce the change they seek. When this creates bedlam, their response is, "Good strike! I made 'em hear me."

Performance Plateaus are reached by the Troublemaker when they: are overzealous to the point of alienating team members, use "below the belt" tactics that backfire, destroy alliances, fail to know when to withdraw, or when they otherwise get in over their heads. One of their major Auto-Reactions is to fault and blame others. They are so accustomed to using blame in their approaches that they often fail to recognize its presence. The Troublemaker's Auto-Reactions say, "They are wrong. I am right and I have rights." They believe that "righting the wrong" brings resolution whether or not this is true in a given situation. Like the Responsible One, they define the parameters of right and wrong in relation to the conditions or situation they hope to correct.

A major flaw in the "right/wrong" thinking of the Troublemaker is that they often define what is right with disregard to the thoughts and viewpoints of others. Although this holds true for almost all of us, it can become extreme in the Troublemaker. When confronted with opposing reality or factual information which emphatically demonstrates their error, they will increase their blame since they have difficulty in accepting that they could be wrong. This, in itself, can create a Performance Plateau because self-correction in midcourse can be quite difficult for them.

Essence:

May long to be at ease, be heard or have others look out for them.

The Clown/Funny One Role

The Clown/Funny One* OFTEN HAS A COMBINATION OF ROLES: Absorber, Renegade, Peacemaker, Caretaker or other subroles. Humor can be used to divert attention, draw attention, relieve tension, avoid chastisement, deflect responsibility, gain favor or cover a multitude of sins. The Clown/Funny One can be very responsible because of their deep-seated fear of rejection or punishment. They may have learned as a child to use humor to deflect the family's attention away from pain and anger. This will be dependent upon the programming which preceded the acceptance or choice of the role of Clown. They seek to prove their value or their professed truth, albeit in a somewhat irreverent manner.

The subconscious program of the Clown/Funny One often seeks to avoid doing what is expected of them because, in their thinking, the expectations are unacceptable or too much work. They seek to gain attention that will bring acceptance. In either posture, responsible or irresponsible, being the Clown/Funny One permits behaviors and statements that might otherwise be unacceptable or punishable. When used by a child, humor clouds issues for others and makes the Clown/Funny One feel more confident since he or she may then gain the loyalty of others, make entry when their guard is down, redirect attention from an issue or disperse focus for convenience.

When alone, the Clown can be very lonely. This loneliness and separation from others makes them prone to procrastination. They may exhibit an ongoing search for that which will bring genuine happiness as

* Those who choose being a comedian as a profession are not included in this discussion.

they concurrently resist change because of potential further discomfort. Often easily discouraged, the Clown/Funny One is prone to run away from wearisome work, avoid direct confrontation and sidestep volatile situations. When they consider you a friend, they can be extremely loyal. However, if that loyalty is exploited or betrayed, it is extremely difficult, if not impossible, to regain their confidence.

The Performance Plateau occurs when the team grows weary of what appears to be a lack of serious investment, forcing the Clown to be genuine and persistent with assignments. If they are programmed to be responsible, a malcontentedness may arise from their own inner conflict which splits their intent. They then have Auto-Reactions which compel responsible behavior at the same time their humor seeks to lighten the drive for supreme responsibility. The CRS says, "Everybody loves me when I'm funny." Exploring deeper feelings are generally avoided. Humor can be a masked pretense that all is well. Actually, the jokes and wittiness are hiding an underlying bitterness or pain that translates to blaming-anger under stress or pressure, and especially in the presence of a Performance Plateau.

Essence:

May long to be the "straight man with a straight assignment."

The Stupid/Dumb One

The Stupid/Dumb One has a difficult role to fulfill. They can be brilliant, yet get assigned a role that requires making foolish mistakes or taking preposterous actions. Expectations are that they will never be skillful, never accomplish or achieve as well as others, never give peak performances. They get caught in the trap of trying to prove their competence in order to dispel this untruth, but seem unable to pull it off. Auto-Reactions compel them to continue in the role of at least *appearing* incompetent in some aspect of their conduct.

The Stupid/Dumb One can be very skilled and appear to have it all together to the onlooker. They may qualify for and land the optimal job. They may actually do a superb job at implementing projects. As they execute the assigned tasks, though, somewhere along the way they will self-sabotage, dig their own grave, so to speak. Because these people are intellectually bright in the presence of sabotaging Auto-Reactions which substantiate their assigned role, the ego can become rather encompassing. They know they are not stupid since they can see achievement in various aspects of their work and their life. The ego, therefore, seeks to counter how they are perceived by others. They can often "have an angle" that will outwit the competition or the boss.

Usually others can see that the Stupid/Dumb One is not dumb at all. In fact, peers may wonder why they so consistently cripple their own position. The Performance Plateau comes when Auto-Reactions cause the Stupid/Dumb One to blunder, to behave in an inefficient manner, to engage in egotistic behaviors, or when their reactive behavior outweighs their conscious desire to perform in an intelligent, innovative and competent manner. Although they have the capacity to absorb and actualize ideas, the CRS says, "You deserve better than this. They are the stupid ones." This renders them careless or engenders unreasonable conscious thinking that further jeopardizes their position. At the same time they are consciously asking themselves, "Why did I do such a stupid thing?" All this translates into endless blame and shame. There is painful shame when alone, but blame overrides the shame in the presence of others because of the strong ego.

Essence:
May long to quit, have less responsibility or be on their own.

The Quiet One Role

The Quiet One can be very smart, almost always focused, deliberate in their actions and particularly observant. They generally are willing to do what is asked or required of them but can also be quite stubborn. Others tend to overlook their doggedness which they quietly use to their own advantage. Frequently, the Quiet One has chosen silence or minimal sharing as a defense prior to getting the role assignment. If others do not know your thoughts or feelings, you gain the upper hand. In addition, silence provides the opportunity to collect information that may be helpful down the road. These people frequently prefer to work alone and can be successful because of their focus. This enables them to accomplish a lot in a short period of time. The Quiet One can be very persistent which enables them to handle long-term goals as long as they have the desire. The tendency is to have a few close team members or friends and spend time almost exclusively with them.

Quietness does not equate peace and calm. These individuals can feel intense fear, shame, blame or guilt. They hold family or business secrets but fear they should not. In their thinking, they often should be able to hold things together for everyone. They see themselves as less than valuable when unable to make bad situations good. Fear that they are "the problem" presents itself in interesting ways, such as becoming reclusive, "hiding out" by reading, spending long hours at a computer or in front of a television set. Though this may happen, their work assignments do not necessarily go unattended. They seem to be enlivened by engaging in stimulating or challenging intellectual activities, preferably alone.

Sometimes, the Quiet One is silent when speaking out or taking a stand would be beneficial. Their fear may hold them back.

A Performance Plateau may come when a high profile is necessary for the task at hand, or when being forced to maintain a visibly active role or prominent showing with a team. Since the CRS says, "Keep a low profile, or else," accepting promotions or assignments that require a public display of their competence or ability may be foreboding. Taking such a risk can mean confronting some very old, very deep fears regarding who they are and what they are permitted to do openly. If there is failure, dealing with significant shame and guilt will be a very real issue.

Essence:

May long to stand up for themselves openly and often, or may just want be left alone.

The Protected One Role

The Protected One has been safeguarded and given emotional refuge by someone who knew them to be in some way wounded, or feared they could be potentially harmed by others. Because of this defense on their behalf, they learn that they need others to button down their security, albeit at a subconscious level. The Protected One learns that they have rights although they must be careful not to be in a position that permits others taking advantage of them. The message recorded in the CRS is two-fold. On one hand, they deserve the very best and must have it, even if in secret. On the other hand, they must always be on the alert, wondering when an adversary might attack. Therefore, they are constantly in a dilemma. Phrases such as "I want to experience or do this," vs. "I must be careful because. . . ," fill their thinking, making life rather perplexing at times.

The Protected One will apply their skills toward achieving a goal and usually do quite well. The problem is that restlessness soon emerges, especially if the situation is tedious or the job is in some way consistently demanding without immediate rewards. When difficult circumstances develop, the Protected One will figure out how to walk away so as not to get hurt or be forced to "take the heat." At the same time, they are skilled at getting others to help them. This means that movement is seen overall as desirable. After all, they are being helped and supported.

Since these individuals have always been protected, they will often, in adulthood, wear a cloak of self-protection. It can be difficult to reach them on a deep level, and some Protected Ones have difficulty being genuinely intimate. Many, though, can be reached with persistence and loyalty. Because of their own experiences, they are also exceptionally well versed in giving assistance to others. Once trust is established, there can be a benevolent exchange of energy or other tradeoffs.

The Performance Plateau for the Protected One is seen when the task at hand continues to be daunting, the rewards are insufficient, no immediate gain can be seen, or the individual is clearly bored with the constancy of the stress or tediousness of the situation. Sticking with the task beyond this point creates an internal struggle. Because their CRS says, "I don't have to endure this," they are placed in a repetitious search for the illusive safe harbor. There is a tendency to succumb to their fears as they step away from the perseverance. The fear of potential backlash or retribution is real, but the Protected One will go beyond them in order to get something better or find that safe harbor. They can be pushed into making these decisions by their Auto-Reactions. The fear of being stuck in an insecure situation, such as a job that doe not pay well, is too much to bear.

As the Protected One moves from experience to experience, they may appear to be unreliable to others. Their tendency to hide out or to take time for themselves contributes to this. However, they can be consistently available to those whom they trust and befriend. Even if they prefer not to, they can also, when necessary, take responsibility for their own welfare. Usually, though, they fight having to do it all.

Essence:

May long for rest, quiet and the perfect job or sanctuary.

Fundamentals

Assigned roles and labels often run our lives or control our behavior

Aside from family roles, we are also nearly constantly labeled by other individuals, groups, clubs, media and so forth. Our behavior, looks, dress, position, automobile, career, body weight, character, jokes, diet, home orderliness, competence, almost everything about us is judged and subsequently labeled. Although people are not necessarily good or bad, better or worse than those around them, labels are assigned.[29] If these labels or roles coincide with or parallel those already programmed in the CRS, there is additional clout in the Auto-Reactions. We may come to believe their validity and they are perpetuated. A Performance Set-Point may be reached sooner than it would have been reached, given these additional external, current-day characterizations.

Recognizing and validating personal roles and labels can be difficult. Yet this is a significantly rewarding aspect of going *Beyond Best*. Self-knowledge and self-awareness creates immeasurable personal power. This holds particularly true when we make Cellular Response System modifications which more completely support and reflect our chosen role(s). In addition, we have the option of creating the clarity and freedom to live beyond restrictive assigned roles.

Appendix

"Even in the grimmest of circumstances, a shift in perspective can create startling change."

-Susan Griffin

I HOPE THAT IN READING *BEYOND BEST* YOU HAVE GAINED insight into some of your programs which cause you to perform in ways you wish to avoid or which create unwanted Auto-Reactions. By now, you understand the necessity of reprogramming those imprints. Many of the lesser driving beliefs can be eliminated with simple exercises. Some of the broader, more encompassing beliefs may need other procedures, and yet others may beg for assistance aside from your own efforts. You can be the judge of that as you experiment with reprogramming.

Numerous programs, techniques, exercises and directives are available to help you change your imprints. Some are simple. Others require more focus from you. I emphasize that certain Auto-Reactions, Set-Points and Role imprints may require outside help because of their complexity. Whether you choose to get assistance can depend upon your goals in relation to change and personal growth.

You will find numerous exercises and various other methods for effecting personal transformation in my book, *Puppet or Puppeteer: Choose The Life You Want To Live, A Companion Guidebook.* In my source book *Puppet or Puppeteer: Choose the Life You Want To Live,* there is a wealth of information regarding personal growth, along with suggestions, instructions, common-sense answers, recommendations for personalizing your reprogramming, and understanding your individual patters and beliefs. Both books are available at **www.AwesomePress.com**. You can also find additional information regarding seminars, workshops, personal sessions, CDs, links to other countermeasures, amazing transforming techniques, and more at **www.AwesomePress.com** or **www.GoBeyondBest.com**.

About the Author

AT AGE 39, NELL RESIGNED FROM A PRESTIGIOUS POSITION at a state training and research facility. She made a radical decision to give away most of her possessions, said good-bye to friends, and traveled, hiking the wilderness across America. After more than a year of exploring, she found answers, but more importantly, discovered herself. In so doing, she made the decision to help others learn how to tap into their core selves.

Over the past 30 years, Dr. Nell has been a speaker of truth while at the same time helping thousands of others along their journey to an inspired life. Her books, *Puppet or Puppeteer: Choose the Life You Want to Life* and *Puppet or Puppeteer: Choose The Life You Want To Live - A Companion Guidebook*, have been bestsellers on Amazon.com. Her programs have made her a sought-after speaker across the world.

Dr. Nell has been an associate professor on a university faculty and served as a registered nurse, a psychotherapist, and as a doctor of chiropractic in her private holistic health practice. Her humor, skills, compassion and knowledge have made her a sought-after lecturer, clinician and consultant. Her kindness, sensitivity and giving spirit is readily apparent as she implements and teaches her down-to-earth, practical programs. Her suggestions and prescriptions for healing lives are based in experience and a broad education combined with gentleness, honor and respect for others. She actively practices what she preaches and firmly believes that we are charged with the responsibility of fulfilling our potential, be it mother/father, trash collector, doctor, entrepreneur or artist. In that regard, she has an uncanny ability to see the essence of those she encounters and to encourage individuals to believe in themselves. Because of her tenacious persistence and commitment, she has acquired a breadth of experience and knowledge far beyond that of the average professional.

Early in her career, Dr. Nell was presented the "Outstanding Nurse" medal, an award created by a hospital medical staff as a means of honoring her contributions. She has never looked back.

Her steadfast invitation to others is: "Live Big!"

End Notes

1. Lipton, Bruce, *The Biology of Belief: Unleashing the Power of Consciousness, Matter and Miracles*, Mountain of Love/Elite Books, Santa Rosa, CA, 2005, p. 15.

2. <http://www.bbc.co.uk>, Science & Nature, TV & Radio Follow-Up, Programmes, Horizon.

3. Nijhout, H. F., "Metaphors and the Role of Genes in Development," *Bioessays*, 1990, 12: p. 442.

4. Eker, T. Harv, *Secrets of the Millionaire Mind: Mastering the Inner Game of Wealth,* Harper Business, New York, 2005, p. 17.

5. <http://www.m-w.com> Merriam-Webster Online.

6. Pert, Candace, *Molecules of Emotion: The Science Behind Mind-Body Medicine*, Touchstone, New York, 1997, p. 145.

7. ibid, p. 144.

8. ibid, p. 143.

9. Neubauer, David, "Reconstructing Memories: Trust, But Verify," *Johns Hopkins Medicine Post*, 2006, p. 1.

10. Walker, Scott, "N.E.T. Glossary," *NET Certification Manual*, Encinitas, CA, 1996, p. 144.

11. Private Client.

12. Singer, Blair, *Code of Honor, Sales Dogs Training School*, Amazon Audio, Phoenix, AZ, Tape 6.

13. Collins, Jim, *Good to Great*, Random House Business Books, New York, 2001.

14. Eichenwald, Kurt, *Conspiracy of Fools: A True Story*, Broadway Reprints, New York, 2005.

15. Hill, Napoleon, *Think and Grow Rich*, Ballantine Books, New York, 1987.

16. Peter, Laurence J., *The Peter Principle*, Buccaneer Books, Cuthogue, NY, 1993.

17. Clance, Pauline, *The Imposter Phenomenon: Overcoming the Fear That Haunts Your Success*, Peachtree Publishing Ltd., Atlanta, GA, 1985, p. 183.

18. <http://www.peanutscollectorclub.com/football.html> November 14, 1951, strip.

19. Gerald Posner, *Citizen Perot: His Life and Times*, Random House, New York, 1996, p. 128.

20. Pert, op. cit., p. 147.

21. <http://www.Oprah.com> Faith Hill & Lori.

22. Ray, Michael, *The Highest Goal: The Secret That Sustains You in Every Moment*, Berrett-Koehler, San Francisco, 2005, p. 34.

23. Epstein, Mark, *Going on Being: Buddhism and the Way of Change: A Positive Psychology for the West*, Broadway Books, New York, 2001, p. 135.

24. Roy, Arundhati, *The God of Small Things*, Harper Perennial, New York, 1998, p. 129.

25. Lipton, op. cit., p. 165.

26. Williamson, Porter, *Patton's Principles: A Handbook for Managers Who Mean It*, Touchtone, New York, 1982, p.164.

27. Kornfield, Jack, *A Path With A Heart: A Guide Through The Perils and Promises of Spiritual Life*, Bantam, New York, p. 283.

28. Pogo, strip from Earth Day, Copyright 1971, 2005 OGPI.

29. Rodgers, Nell, *Puppet or Puppeteer: Choose the Life You Want to Live*, Awesome Press, Decatur, GA, p. 284.

Selected Bibliography

Armstrong, Alison A., *Keys to the Kingdom*, PAX Programs Incorporated, Sherman Oaks, CA, 2003.

Bandler, Richard and Grinder, John, *Frogs Into Princes: Neuro-Linguistic Programming*, Real People Press, Moab, Utah, 1979.

Bandler, Richard, *Using Your Brain for a Change: Neuro-Linguistic Programming*, Real People Press, Moab, Utah, 1985.

Benson, Herbert and Klipper, Miriam A., *The Relaxation Response*, Harper Collins, New York, 2000.

Borysenko, Joan, *Guilt Is the Teacher, Love Is the Lesson*, Warner Books, New York, 1991.

Bronson, Po, *What Should I Do With My Life: The True Story of People Who Answered the Ultimate Question*, Random House Trade Paperbacks, New York, 2003.

Cameron, Julia, *The Artist's Way: A Spiritual Path to Higher Creativity*, Jeremy P. Tarcher/Perigee Books, New York, 1992.

Catford, Lorena and Ray, Michael, *The Path of the Everyday Hero*, Tarcher-Putnam, New York, 1991.

Chopra, Deepak, *The Spontaneous Fulfillment of Desire*, Harmony Books, New York, 2003.

Covey, Stephen R., *7 Habits of Highly Effective People: Powerful Lessons in Personal Change*, Simon and Schuster, New York, 1989.

Dyer, Wayne W., *The Power of Intention: Learning to Co-Create Your World Your Way*, Hay House, Carlsbad, CA, 2004.

______, *When You Believe It You Will See It: The Way to Your Personal Transformation*, William Morrow and Co., Inc., New York, 1989.

Ford, Debbie, *The Dark Side of the Light Chasers: Reclaiming Your Power, Creativity, Brilliance and Dreams*, Riverhead Books, New York, 1998.

Gandhi, (Mahatma) Mohandas K., *An Autobiography: The Story of My Experiments with Truth*, Beacon Press, Boston, 1957.

Gerber, Richard, *Vibrational Medicine: New Choices for Healing Ourselves*, Bear & Co., Santa Fe, NM, 1988.

Gibson, Lindsay, *Who You Were Meant to Be*, New Horizon Press, Far Hills, NJ, 2000.

Gilbert, Roberta, *Extraordinary Relationships: A New Way of Thinking About Human Interactions*, Wiley, New York, 1992.

Gladwell, Malcolm, *Blink: The Power of Thinking Without Thinking*, Bay Back Books, Boston, 2007.

Goleman, Daniel, Kaufman, Paul and Ray, Michael, *The Creative Spirit,* Dutton, New York, 1991.

Goleman, Daniel, *Emotional Intelligence: Why It Can Matter More Than IQ*, Bantam Books, New York, 1995.

Griscom, Chris, *The Healing of Emotion: Awakening the Fearless Self*, Light Institute Press, Galisteo, NM, 1999.

Hay, Louise, *Heal Your Body A-Z: The Mental Causes for Physical Illness and the Way to Overcome Them*, Hay House, Carlsbad, CA, 1998.

Justice, Blair, *Who Gets Sick: How Beliefs, Moods and Thoughts Affect Your Health*, Jeremy P. Tarcher, Inc., Los Angeles, 1987.

McGraw, Phillip C., *Self Matters: Creating Your Life From the Inside Out*, Simon & Schuster, New York, 2001.

Miller, Alice, *The Drama of the Gifted Child: The Search for the True Self*, Basic Books, New York, 1996.

Mipham, Sakyong and Chadron, Pema, *Turning the Mind Into an Ally*, Riverhead Books, New York, 2003.

Pearson, Carol S., *The Hero Within: Six Archetypes We Live By*, HarperSanFrancisco, San Francisco, 1998.

Peters, Thomas J. and Waterman, Robert H., *In Search of Excellence*, Reprint, Collins, New York, 2004.

Rodgers, Nell, *Puppet or Puppeteer: Companion Guidebook*, Awesome Press, Decatur, GA, p. 140.

Rosenberg, Marshall B., *Nonviolent Communication: A Language of Compassion*, Puddle Dancer Press, Encinitas, CA, 1999.

Saloff, Jamie L., *Transformational Healing: Five Surprisingly Simple Keys Designed to Redirect Your Life, Toward Wellness, Purpose and Prosperity*, Sent Books, Edinboro, PA, 2005.

Selye, Hans, *The Stress of Life*, McGraw-Hill Book Company, New York, 1956.

Shapiro, Francine, *EMDR: The Breakthrough Therapy for Overcoming Anxiety, Stress and Trauma*, Basic Books, New York, 1997.

Sher, Barbara and Smith, Barbara, *I Could Do Anything If I Only Knew What It Was*, Dell Publishing, New York, 1994.

Smith, Hyrum W., *What Matters Most: The Power of Living Your Values*, Fireside Rockefeller Center, New York, 2000.

Sultenfuss, Sylvia, *The Joy of Adulthood*, Palladium Press, Atlanta, GA, 2004.

Tracy, Brian, *Create Your Own Future: How to Master the 12 Critical Factors of Unlimited Success*, John Wiley & Sons, New York, 2002.

Vamos, Mark, Editor, *Fast Company Magazine*, New York, <http://www.fastcompany.com>.

Walker, Scott, "Ivan Pavlov, His Dog and Chiropractic," *The Digest of Chiropractic Economics*, March/April, 1992.

Walker, Scott, "Once More With Feeling," *The Digest of Chiropractic Economics*, May/June, 1990.

Williams, Robert M., *Psych-K: The Missing Peace in Your Life*, Spirit 2000, Inc. Publications, Memphis, TN, 2002.

Zukav, Gary, *The Seat of The Soul*, Simon and Schuster, New York, 1989.

www.ingramcontent.com/pod-product-compliance
Lightning Source LLC
LaVergne TN
LVHW050630100826
845148LV00011B/1809

* 9 7 8 0 9 7 4 5 2 4 0 3 0 *